vivacious Curvy Quilts

DIANNE S. HIRE

American Quilter's Society
P. O. Box 3290 • Paducah, KY 42002-3290
www.AmericanQuilter.com

Located in Paducah, Kentucky, the American Quilter's Society (AQS) is dedicated to promoting the accomplishments of today's quilters. Through its publications and events, AQS strives to honor today's quiltmakers and their work and to inspire future creativity and innovation in quiltmaking.

EXECUTIVE BOOK EDITOR: ANDI MILAM REYNOLDS
GRAPHIC DESIGN: ELAINE WILSON
COVER DESIGN: MICHAEL BUCKINGHAM
QUILT PHOTOGRAPHY: CHARLES R. LYNCH, *unless otherwise noted*
HOW-TO PHOTOGRAPHY: TERRY HIRE

Additional copies of this book may be ordered from the American Quilter's Society, PO Box 3290, Paducah, KY 42002-3290, or online at www.AmericanQuilter.com.

Text © 2010, Author, Dianne S. Hire
Artwork © 2010, American Quilter's Society

Library of Congress Cataloging-in-Publication Data

Hire, Dianne S.
    Vivacious curvy quilts / by Dianne S. Hire.
        p. cm.
    Includes index.
    ISBN 978-1-57432-674-1
    1. Quilting. 2. Quilts--Design. 3. Patchwork--Design. I. Title.
    TT835.H53345 2010
    746.46'041--dc22

                        2010035272

TITLE PAGE: FRISBEE FLING, detail, full quilt page 53

Proudly printed and bound in the
United States of America

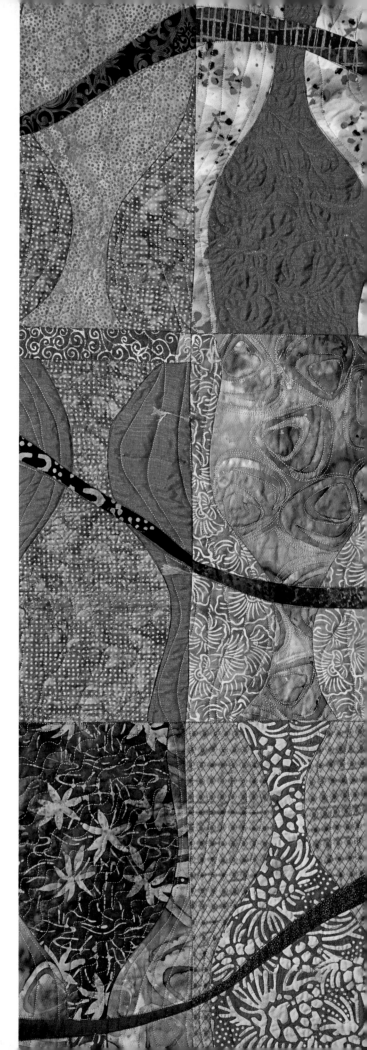

Dedication

To Mom, who never, ever said that I couldn't.

To friends, who put up with so many nutty ideas.

To quiltmakers, who continue to spark the fire to make ideas happen.

To AQS, for patience with the longest running writing contract in history.

To Sir Hilary, who creatively combines fabrics in ways that only cats can.

And, of course, to all *children-at-heart* who trust me enough and are willing to play curvaceously along. May we always be child-adults just as Antoine de Saint-Exupéry in *The Little Prince* described: "Grown-ups never understand anything for themselves, and it is tiresome for children to be always and forever explaining things to them." May we never lose our attitude of childlike play.

But finally, mostly, and always, *always...*

To Terry, who encourages and loves me in spite of myself.

ABOVE: **Sir Hilary**

LEFT: **Broken Vessels**, detail, full quilt page 27

Contents

OPPOSITE AND RIGHT: STARRY, STARRY NIGHTS, details,
full quilt on page 88

Foreword
by Laura Wasilowski

Dianne Hire is a delight and this delight is reflected in her art work. Bright colors, innovative use of fabric, and meandering, swirling, twirling, movement describe her style. No dull quilts here.

Over the years, I've appreciated Dianne's wizardry with color and elegant embellishment. She takes a simple block and turns it on its head. She takes a wallflower color and makes it sing. Her playful trademark style is always a treat and leaves me asking for more.

I am also witness to Dianne's patient and positive instruction as a teacher. Her ability to impart the art of improvisational design and transfer the joy of working with color is found in the classroom as well as in this book.

So enjoy your visit with Dianne! Bring on the fun!

Laura Wasilowski
laura@artfabrik.com

LEFT: SAPPHIRE, detail, full quilt on page 85

Vivacious Curvy Quilts ● DIANNE S. HIRE

Introduction

t was my preference for nontraditional, unlikely quilt shapes and improvisational methods that kept curves out of my quilt life. It goes against my grain (okay, brain) to intricately measure and mark seam allowances, much less try to sew those scary curves—and when I did, the disastrous results had strange and bubbly seams.

Either I meticulously basted the continuous line prior to sewing or I tortured myself with overuse of a seam ripper's pointy little end. So it was that for years I steered clear of any curvy seams or inset curves. Too hard…too intricate…too many pins… and for me, too much time wasted.

Then came one of those "Aha!" moments. I watched a friend easily steer her sewing machine in and around a difficult curve and light bulbs flashed with the discovery of ways to use this technique. Since so many of our traditional blocks are pieced in curves, I thought, "Why not use the same kind of non-template piecing that another of my AQS books, *Quilters Playtime,* enjoyed?"

About my previous difficulty with curves, the truth is, I could never remember which curve is concave or convex. With my vivacious curvy techniques, you don't need to know which piece is curved like the inner surface of a sphere (that defines concave) or which piece has a boundary that bulges outward (that's convex).

I hope that you find reading and sewing from *Vivacious Curvy Quilts* as much fun as I had writing it. I'm loving the methods that create the curvy shapes and keep discovering more and more uses for them. You'll find this book as much a technique and process book as a "make that project" book, so keep your heart open and let your imagination be your guide. ENJOY!

LEFT: CLASS CLOWN, detail, full quilt on page 46

chapter 1
Getting Started

By giving overall instructions to create a block yet leaving out any set dimensions or specific light-medium-dark color sets, I believe that quiltmakers will find the freedom to explore new and different ways to implement the given instructions for these projects. My thought is this: *have at it!* Go for whatever makes your heart happy. Your own creativity will be examined, explored, and further celebrated.

In the final analysis, it seems to me that you are limited by two things: your own imagination and your supply of fabrics, budget included. Where both of those take you is really up to you. I find myself always amazed at what quiltmakers dream up. Dreaming and imagining is easy. As always, it is the dream's execution toward which we constantly strive. I hope this book helps you find ways to execute some of those dreams.

Overview and Fabric Selection

First off, let's get this out in the open: for this improvisational method of sewing curves, your seam allowances **must be ⅛",** not ¼".

Throughout this book, you will read about "curvies," my nickname for the technique.

Your two best friends are the iron and a spray water bottle (Fig. 1–1). By using these best friends, nearly always and sometimes with a little gentle coercion, most of the troubling issues that some curves offer may be avoided.

> **Hint:** For successful seams sewn with a ⅛" seam allowance, drop your stitch length to much less than the normal 12-14 stitches per inch. Use 60 wt. cotton embroidery thread for piecing. It is great in the bobbin because you can load more thread, thus fewer stops before another bobbin fill.

Fact: It is to our advantage that most fabrics have the quality of maneuverability. Since some fabric curvies fall into place very nicely whereas some totally refuse to play anywhere near nicely, we benefit from that trait. Those bad-guy-curvies may be pushed, shoved, and subdued with a spritz of water and an aggressive pressing to insure a nice, evenly dispersed, and shapely line.

In nearly every case, begin with a stack of 4 to 6 fabrics rather than working with only one fabric at a time. Look at the fabrics (Fig. 1–2, page 10). Make sure you like all 4 fabrics together in every possible combination. Next, see if they pass this simple test: Does Fabric A look good with Fabric C? How about Fabric A with Fabric D? Last, view Fabric B with Fabric D (Fig. 1–3, page 10). By asking these questions, you are able to ascertain the compatibility of all 4 fabrics. If one does not make your heart happy, remove it, take it away, put it out of visual range. A change-out is needed.

Fig. 1–1: Iron + water = a fix to straighten most uncooperative curvy seams

OPPOSITE: Curvaceous Squares, detail, full quilt on page 16

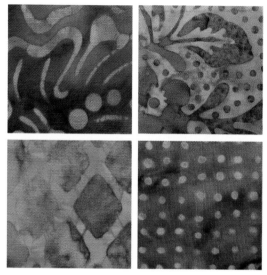

Fig. 1–2: Select 4 fabrics that you would put together as if making a normal quilt.

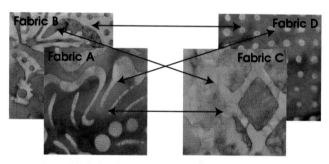

Fig. 1–3: Look at the way the 4 fabrics are stacked 2 plus 2, but off-centered. By viewing these four as a potential set rather than as individual fabrics, you can decide whether a change-out is needed.

> **Hint:** When cutting curves with this method, I suggest a rotary cutter with a small blade. I use both an 18mm blade and one that is a bit larger—about ½" in diameter. The smaller the blade, the easier it is to control and rotate the cut.

Supplies and Tools

Have on hand:

- a clean, well-oiled sewing machine
- a regular sewing foot that gives a larger holding surface than the ¼" foot
- neutral threads (gray or off-white); it is optional, but my preference for piecing is 60 wt. embroidery thread.
- water bottle for spritzing
- iron and ironing surface
- comfortable chair
- rotary-cutting tools
- same-size fabric squares (100% cotton) that may be cut anywhere from 4" to 7", as many as you wish as long as you like the group's color combinations
- scissors to clean-finish your seams
- small kitchen tongs (optional)

If you are nervous about using a rotary cutter freeform without the protection of a plastic ruler's edge, you can protect your fingers by placing a small pair of kitchen tongs between your forefinger and third finger. Hold this protective device at the same time you are pushing down the stack of fabrics with your non-cutting hand (Fig. 1–4).

Fig. 1–4: Tongs protect your fingers as you slide the rotary cutter along the fabric to make a graceful curvy cut.

Types of Cuts

There are several types of cuts for your curvies. Overall, and as a general guideline, curvy cuts should be gentle in shape rather than harsh or sharp (Figs. 1–5a–c). The opposite is also true; a flat, unattractive curve is created if the curve does not have enough gentle shapeliness to it. Also, to accomplish a really good gentle curve, make your cut so that no part is equal—that nothing is equidistant.

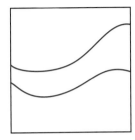 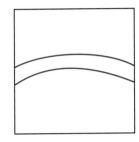 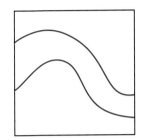

Fig. 1–5a: Try to make gentle curves but nothing equidistant.

Fig. 1–5b: This curve is too flat.

Fig. 1–5c: A sharp curve such as this is more difficult to sew.

Gentle curves make for ease in sewing them together. When sewn together, a sharp curve will be extremely catty-whompus.

Here are sketches of several other types of curvies (Figs. 1–6a–g); I'm certain you will add many more to your repertoire as you treat yourself to this fun technique.

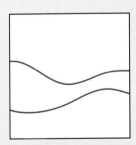 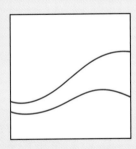 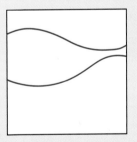 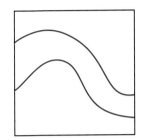

Fig. 1–6a: Graceful curvy

Fig. 1–6b and c: Pointy left and pointy right curves

Fig. 1–6d: Vase or vessel curvy

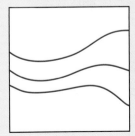 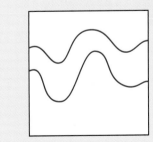

Fig. 1–6e and f: Double curvy and multiple curvy

Fig. 1–6g: California 101, a lovely and gentle cut, but more difficult to create. I submit: it is almost impossible without hand piecing the curve.

Flat Pressing

Create a 4-fabric set by pressing all 4 fabrics together. First, press the bottom fabric onto the ironing surface. Layer the next fabric aligning it *exactly* on top of the last one; press both together. Layer the 3rd fabric *precisely* on top of both and press again. Lastly, add the 4th fabric, taking care to *align with precision* onto the other three; then press. This pressing trick makes a nicely flattened unit and as such will yield more accurate rotary cutting when working with stacked fabrics.

Spritz and press after each seam is sewn. Further, **always** spritz using the water bottle **before** you press seams to one side. By adhering to this general rule, you will be able to "fix" any bubbly, wavy, yucky seams before you wade into deeper waters. *Don't wait until the entire block is sewn before pressing.* Please. Additionally, you may find it helpful to set the seam first before pressing to one side.

What happens if you get what I call a blobble— a seam that absolutely will not lie flat? Simply press out any extra fabric(s) to make the seam lie flat (it is possible, you know). Then follow the newly pressed line as a guide for a new stitching line on the next seam. Compare the blobble with the newly pressed curvy in Figs. 1–7a–d.

Fig. 1–7a: This is an uncooperative blobble.

Fig. 1–7b: This is a pressed-out blobble.

Fig. 1–7c: You can see the seam line along the pressing line.

Fig. 1–7d: The result is a newly sewn curvy.

Lift-and-Separate and Push-and-Pull Basics

A push-and-pull technique that I call "lift-and-separate" is used as you stitch the ⅛" curvy seams. The title is not original; it was an imaginative student who once said, "Oh, just call it the Playtex® method of *lift-and-separate*!!!" Actually, her comment describes the method precisely (Figs. 1–8a–c).

While lifting and separating, you will also exert a gentle push-and-pull movement. The push sends the top fabric onto the bottom one and the ever-so-gentle pull aligns the bottom fabric underneath the top one. When the curve reverses, the pull will be on the top fabric with a little push to align the bottom fabric underneath.

These are simultaneous actions—lift-and-separate, push-and-pull. At first, this is slightly awkward, but after a few curvy blocks you will be rolling along so fast that steam will be coming from your sewing factory. I admit this: making curvies is addictive and easy once you get the knack. You will be looking for new ways to use them, I promise.

Consistency and Production Piecing

It is very important to begin stitching at the same place on every block (Fig. 1–9). I suggest that you lay out the 4 different blocks in this way: always plan to begin your stitching on the left-hand side, whether you are left- or right-handed (Figs. 1–10, page 14).

Fig. 1–8a: Lift: As you are sewing 2 curved fabrics together, always hold the top fabric in your left hand while maneuvering the bottom fabric with your right hand.

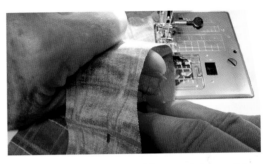

Fig. 1–8b: Lift: The top fabric is lying softly over your left thumb.

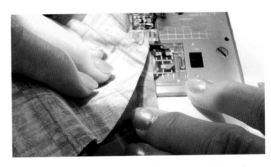

Fig. 1–8c: Separate: Gently manipulate the bottom fabric with your right fingers.

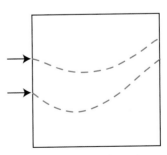

Fig. 1–9: By always sewing from the same starting point on the left, your blocks will be more consistent in shape.

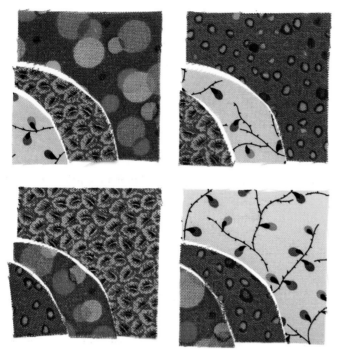

Fig. 1–10: Lay out 4 sets of 3 fabrics. Begin by assigning numbers to each of the 3 pieces in the block. More information on sewing the blocks together is given as you proceed to the next chapter.

Stringing your sewn pieces together in a production-piecing method assures more consistency in your blocks (Fig. 1–11a). Also, this will help you remember to always begin sewing at the same place, doing the same process for all of the blocks (Fig. 1–11b).

After you have pieced the first portion of the 4 units using a production-piecing method, press the seams. I suggest that you press toward the center (inserted) piece (Fig. 1–11c). The reason is so that the inserted center will pop toward you rather than recede away. It matters not if the dark fabric isn't the center piece.

After completing the last seam of all 4 units, again press toward the center (inserted) piece (Fig. 1–12).

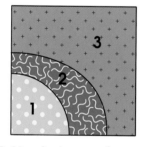

Fig. 1–11a: Assign numbers to every fabric layout.

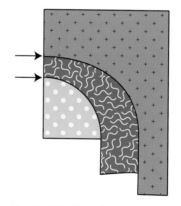

Fig. 1–11b: Sew both seams, always beginning on the left.

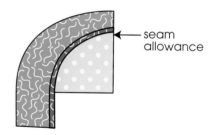

seam allowance

Fig. 1–11c: This is the back of the block with the seam pressed toward the center insert.

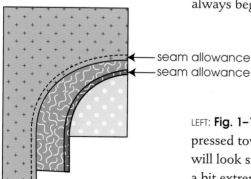

seam allowance
seam allowance

LEFT: Fig. 1–12: When you view the block's back, see how both seams are pressed toward the center to make it pop. Your catty-whompus block will look similar to this and cannot be evenly matched. This drawing is a bit extreme, but your block will get skewed when sewn. This is OK.

Quilter: Walk Away from the Rotary Cutter!

Here's a major quiltdom truth: quiltmakers just love having blocks with nice straight lines and beautifully connected seams; thus we are always tempted to square up a block.

But here's another truth and this one is for curvy-cut blocks: the blocks that you will be creating will be out-of-whack and will always be catty-whompus. It is the nature of curvy-cut blocks. This is OK.

Before you submit to your straight-line cravings, no matter how difficult it may be, please resist the urge to square up your blocks.

For this method, just hold on to your horses and please keep your fingers off the rotary cutter and ruler until your sewn-together and *uneven* blocks are fully designed into a quilt top (unsewn) on the wall.

Popper Colors

To complete certain blocks, you may need a "popper" color. For our curvy purposes, a good definition of a popper is a color that acts as a unifying coloring-agent. For example, you may select green as a popper. Green includes every possible shade or hue of green that you can find—forest, apple, lettuce, peacock, chartreuse, lime, and even a few sea blues or lemony-yellows. A block with a large amount of a pale aqua may need a popper of dark forest green, or a dark-colored navy blue block may ask you for a lime green popper.

Often a popper is a wonderful aid to pull together what may appear to be a group of unlikely block combinations in strangely shaped curvies. The squares may look like they will never work into a viable quilt. Not true. It is the popper's job to eliminate any confusing color mixes and pull your quilt together in a lovely combination of curvy shapes.

Not only does the popper unify, making the many diverse blocks cohesive as the squares now hang together well, a popper also adds enough fabric to actually create a finished square or rectangular shape (Fig. 1–13, page 16).

You may not always need a popper. Since I've not a clue as to how your blocks will look, I cannot predict whether you will or will not need one. But as we proceed, more information will be given. You may read about reserving a popper color, meaning that you will not include one specific color as part of the actual block construction. A popper will be the last color (fabric) added in the process.

For clarification, let's define a popper color by example:

- Say you pick red. The color red in my book includes a complete range of red shades. Red might be apple red, fire-engine red, reddish-orange, deep orange-red, true orange, raspberry, hot pink, fuchsia, or reddish-plum.
- Or, let's explore purple as a popper color: purple has the ability to cross over from being magenta, fuchsia, hyacinth, grape, blueberry, violet, or lavender to royal purple.

I tend to run the color gamut to get a widespread array of colorations. I contend that the wider the variety of different shades, hues, and values you incorporate into your piece, the more it will dance, sing, and dazzle. If you limit yourself to only one red, blue, green, or yellow, you fail to explore how a variety of colors can make your quilt sparkle with vitality.

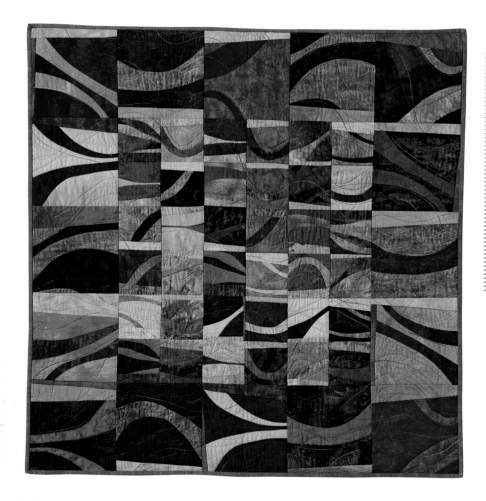

LEFT: **Fig. 1-13:** In CURVACEOUS SQUARES, 39" x 39", made by the author, look at the middle 6 vertical rows before the final borders. Find the green poppers at the bottom of the first row's blocks and at the top of the next row's blocks, alternating across the verticals.

OPPOSITE: STIRRED NOT MIXED, detail, full quilt on page 20

Unmatched Seams

Yes, unmatched seams create a staccato movement in your quilt.

No, they do not ordinarily match.

No, they usually won't line up.

No, you should not fret about it!!!

Yes, get over it and enjoy the vivacious curvy technique.

Open Mind

One of the most important things to have on hand when creating in an intuitive way is an open mind. Over the years we, as quiltmakers, have trained our hands, eyes, and minds to react to a quilt's overall beauty and construction in a certain and very specific way. I search for a word that may best describe that reaction and submit this phrase: "we seek perfection." Whether we look for perfectly aligned points, perfectly shaped squares, and/or perfectly spaced quilting stitches at fewer than 10 to an inch, many of us may admit having become a quilt-snob trying to assess and view a quilt with certain sets of "perfection-driven" parameters.

Although curvies offer an antidote to such a mind-set, we still have a remainder of "perfection" in our quilterly heads. I maintain strongly that every quilter must know the rules of perfection in order to know how best to break them. Thus, an open mind that understands both of those interpretations will be the best to play into these easy and fun curvy construction methods of improv and intuition.

chapter 2
Two-color Curvy Squares

Continuous Curvies

The continuous curvy is probably the easiest of the curvies to learn and to construct. A continuous curvy always connects only to opposite sides of a square. It can be either vertical or horizontal. I suggest that you begin with this one.

No matter whether it is cut horizontally or vertically, the finished block will be the same. You have the option of turning the block, when sewn together, in any direction you want (Figs. 2–1a and b).

Two wonderful uses for this specific curvy are as a border surrounding a quilt or as a traveler that takes your eye in a line across the quilt (Fig. 2–1c).

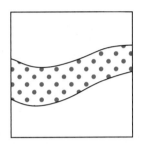

Fig. 2–1a: This is a horizontal continuous curvy.

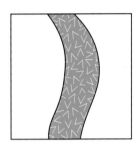

Fig. 2–1b: This is a vertical continuous curvy.

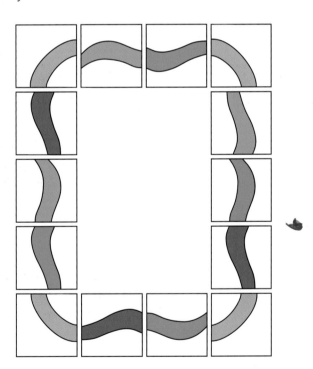

Fig. 2–1c: A continuous-curvy border can be made of opposite side curvies with the exception of the 4 corners. To connect the traveling border, the 4 corners require a circular curvy as shown on pages 32–34.

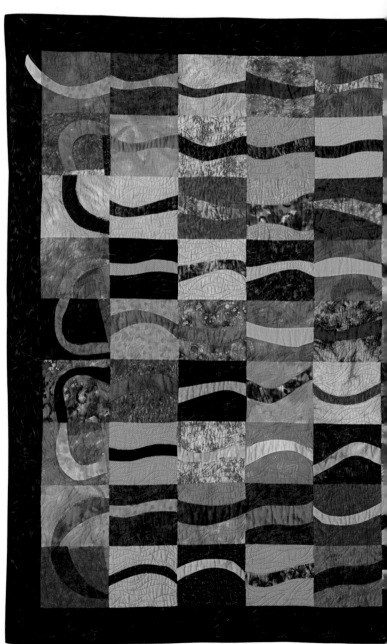

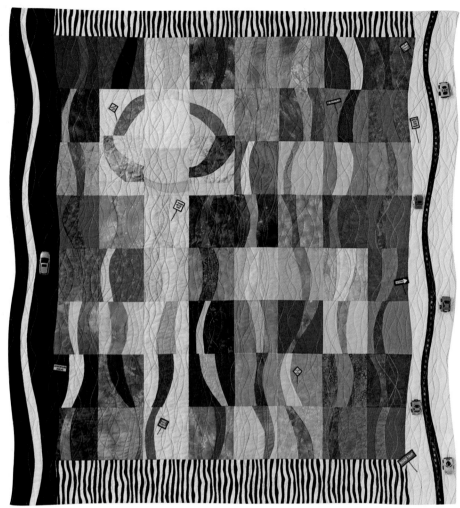

ABOVE: LIFE ON THE TECHNICOLOR HIGHWAY, 57" x 54", made by Jane Lange of Medford, New Jersey, and quilted by Carolyn Ensminger of Lakeside Quilting, includes a rotary to take the cars in a traffic circle.

LEFT: Look at how SWITCHBACK, 67" x 60", designed and made by Sharon Price of Beckley, West Virginia, begins at the top of the design with the blocks horizontally arranged, and just like following a maze or a switchback in a highway, Sharon takes us out of the quilt near the bottom.

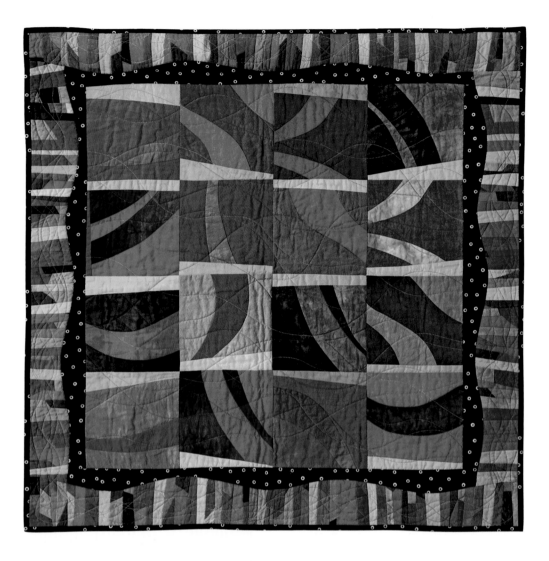

ABOVE: GO WITH THE FLOW, 28" x 28", was made by Kathyl Jogerst of Coralville, Iowa. The black-and-white inner border gives definition to the central 16-block design.

LEFT: Mary Dyer of Merritt Island, Florida, created STIRRED NOT MIXED, 43" x 43", detail page 17, an almost two-color quilt with circular movement in deliciously edible reds and tangerines that offset the blues and purples. Turquoise serves as a color splash.

ABOVE: Janet Myers of Flandreau, South Dakota, created UNTITLED, 41" x 49". It is made up of both continuous curvies and circular curvies (see pages 18 and 32). Notice how the motion frames her piece with refined excitement.

RIGHT: RED LETTER, 33" x 42", made by Conni DeYoung of North Ft. Myers, Florida, has the same continuous curvy arranged in a more random way and is accented with graphic black-and-white checks and dots.

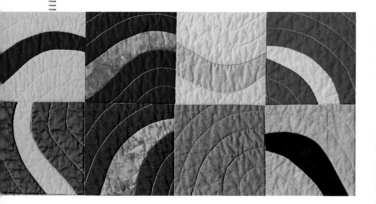

ABOVE, DETAIL BELOW: Katherine L. Miller of Chadron, Nebraska, also used more than one type of curvy for her quilt, HIRER THAN A KITE, 53" x 78". I love the play on my name!

Instructions – Continuous Curvies

To create a continuous curvy vertical or horizontal quilt, select 4 basic fabric colorways, for example, blue, yellow, purple, and green. For your first try, I suggest that you use hand-dyed or similar fabrics that read as solids because they are easy to combine. Find 4 different fabrics from each colorway for a total of 16 different fabrics (Fig. 2–2).

Fig. 2–2: 16 different fabrics (4 blues, 4 yellows, 4 purples, 4 greens)

Note that the color red is not included. Red will be reserved as the popper color and may be used later when you are ready to sew the blocks together. See page 15 (Chapter 1) for more information about poppers.

Cut all 16 fabrics into squares any size you wish from 4" to 7" (Fig. 2–3, page 23). Larger is better if this is your first curvy adventure.

One by one, beginning with the bottom fabric and ending with the top fabric, press each set together to flatten as a unit of 4. Pressing in this way makes for better accuracy when rotary cutting. See page 12 for details on flat pressing.

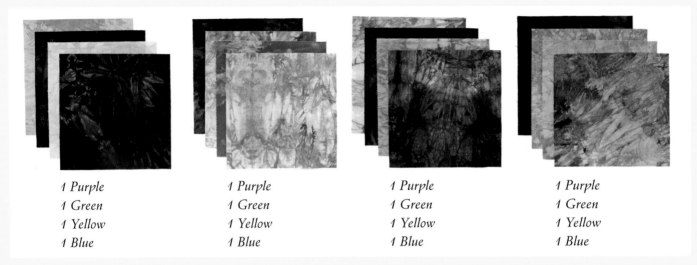

1 Purple
1 Green
1 Yellow
1 Blue

1 Purple
1 Green
1 Yellow
1 Blue

1 Purple
1 Green
1 Yellow
1 Blue

1 Purple
1 Green
1 Yellow
1 Blue

Fig. 2-3: Separate the colors into sets, 1 per foursome.

Carefully place the 4-fabric unit on your rotary-cutting surface. With a very sharp rotary blade make your first continuous curvy cut from one side of the square to the side across from it. Try not to lift the cutter or see-saw as you make your cuts (Fig. 2–4).

Make your second rotary cut. Vary the widths and curvy shapes; the inset curved shape will not be equidistant. Also, a strong curve in a horseshoe shape is more difficult to sew; I suggest that you save that for another day.

Arrange the 4 colors into different blocks by partnering 2 colors with each other (Fig. 2–5). The first partners are blue with green; the second partners are yellow with purple. You will have 4 different blocks but the same color combinations in 2 of the blocks.

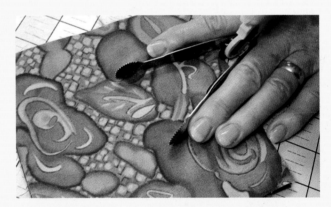

Fig. 2–4: Push the tongs ahead of and with your two fingers as you move the rotary cutter along the fabric.

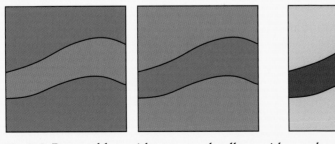

Fig. 2–5: Partner blue with green and yellow with purple.

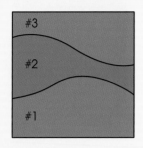

Fig. 2–6: Assign a number to each of the units, i.e., 1, 2 and 3. Sew 2 to 1 then sew 3 to the 2-1 unit. Refer to pages 12–13 about the lift-and-separate and push-and-pull techniques to begin sewing. Reminder: the seam allowance should be ⅛".

Production (or chain) piecing works very well with this method. Whatever you do, repeat for all 4 blocks and do not cut them apart. Assign a number to each of the units, i.e., 1, 2 and 3. Sew 2 to 1 (Fig. 2–6).

As you complete each seam, press toward 2. Sew 3 to the 2-1 unit. Press toward 2. Set these 4 blocks aside.

Hint: Do not cut apart the first string made up of 2 fabrics. Instead, press them while still sewn as 4 strung-together units. This will help remind you where to place these fabrics. Although this may not be very important with 2-color blocks, it will be a very useful hint when you sew together 3-color blocks.

When your first 4 blocks are sewn together, do NOT square up any block yet. You will want to square up the uneven edges, yes, I know, but do not do it now!!!! At this point, you have no idea what the final dimensions of the curvy block will be and you may need every tiny ¹⁄₁₆" increment.

Repeat the rotary cutting, arranging, and sewing of another set (4 different fabrics). Always vary the placement and size of the curve within each set of fabrics until you have completed all 16 blocks.

Resist the temptation to square up or arrange the blocks. *It is best to create a minimum of 24 blocks before designing your wallhanging.*

Suggestion: Select fabrics for 2 more sets of 4 fabrics that coordinate with the first 16 blocks. By sewing more blocks, you will have more options for arranging as you design.

When you have sewn together a minimum of 24 blocks, *if you cannot resist,* begin arranging on the wall. You may place the blocks as travelers, verticals, horizontals, or as borders. Instead, you may decide to make more blocks for a larger wallhanging because 24 blocks aren't very many.

If that is the case, remember, do not square up the blocks until you have completed a full layout of your quilt top's intended design. Look ahead to page 50 to see Laura Christensen working on her design wall. Nothing was "squared up" until all 24 of her component blocks were finished; poppers were laid in place, then added to each component block in the form of a windmill; and her quilt top was completely designed. All of this happened before she squared up anything. It is difficult to resist, but remember, *quilter, walk away from the rotary cutter!*

For the entire quilt, I suggest that at this point you might wish to include different types of blocks, saving these continuous curvies to put with others described in this book for a full assortment. Having more blocks offers you the option to pick and choose, to fill in spaces, and to use some blocks and discard others if the colorations or designs do not work well in combination.

Vessel or Chalice Curvies

Vessels are an excellent way to create 2-color continuous curvies using a rectangle for a beginning point instead of a square. This elongates the design, giving a new dimension to curvies.

By including as many as 4 shapes in your design, active variety is accomplished (Fig. 2–7). Repeating only 1 shape with 16 blocks would be more passive. Depending on your choice, you may soften the quilt by using the same vessel-shaped design. If you opt to do that and to repeat the shape, be sure to make a template of your vessel.

The penciled sketches are purposely shown in gray-scale to allow you freedom in color selection. Can you see how the mixture of color might be manipulated for a wonderful creation?

If you opt to make 4 different vessel shapes for your 16-block design, note that each shape is on a set of 4 stacked fabrics so that when completed, there will be 16 blocks (Fig. 2–8). The fabrics are interchanged within each block.

Another design alternates the vessel shapes (Figs. 2–9 and 10, page 26).

- Row 1 has one upright vessel with the next shape turned downward, then a repeat.
- Row 2 reverses the sequence: one downward, next upright, then repeat.
- Row 3 is the same as Row 1.
- Row 4 is the same as Row 2.

Again, there are 4 sets of 4 stacked fabrics with 4 possible vessel shapes. Why not sketch your own shapes? These are included as samples only. *Go for it!*

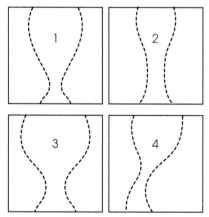

ABOVE: **Fig. 2–7:** Four different vessel shapes, each sitting on 4 different fabrics, are made of side-to-side curvy cuts.

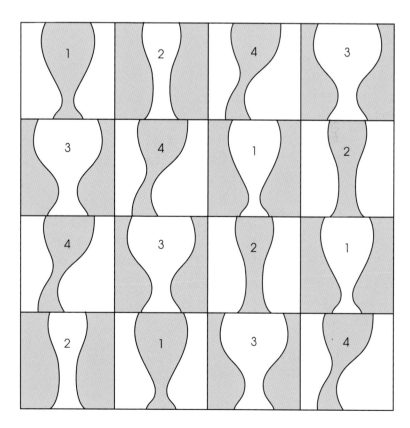

RIGHT: **Fig. 2–8:** Imagine how jewel colors would make this upright vessel shape look with 4 sets of 4 interchanged fabrics.

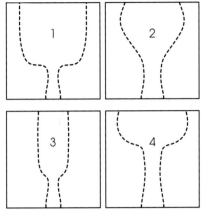

ABOVE: **Fig. 2–9:** If you wish, why not try sketching other vessel shapes?

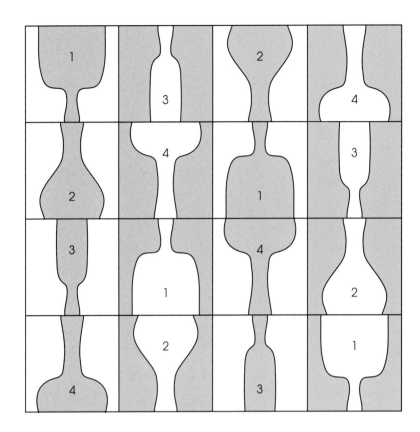

RIGHT: **Fig. 2–10:** Vessels are alternated up and down and in 4 sets of 4 fabrics.

Instructions –
Vessel or Chalice Curvies

I suggest that the best way to create vessels is to design on paper first. Cut 4 paper rectangles approximately 18" x 12"–13". The vessel shape with its very slender stems makes for a bit more difficult stitchery, so a larger format will be easier to sew.

Draw 4 different curvy vessel shapes (Fig. 2–11, page 27). Try to draw gentle shapes that are not too curvy since that will increase the difficulty of stitching. When you are satisfied with each design, cut out the paper vessel and use this as a template.

To create 4 vessels, select 4 fabrics. Each vessel will need a partnership of 2 fabrics, so select your fabrics with that in mind. Use the flat pressing technique on page 12.

Use each paper vessel as a template for each different pairing of fabrics. Place the vessel on the pressed-together pair and follow the lines with your rotary cutter.

Alternate the fabrics and production piece them with the curvy technique as in other units (see pages 22–24).

Press aggressively toward the vessel no matter the fabric colors (light or dark).

Should you wish to keep the vessels intact without breaking apart the vessel design, simply "rectangle-up" (meaning, square-up) the units and sew them together. This, in its simplicity of design, will make a lovely wallhanging.

On the other hand, if you are up to *breaking the vessels*, this, too, is a viable and lovely design. It is also a double use of your newly acquired curvy technique in that the vessels are curved and the break in the vessel is also curved.

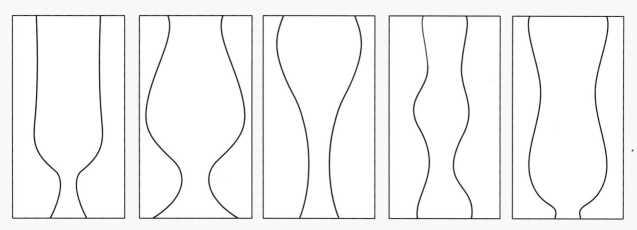

Fig. 2–11: Feel free to enlarge and duplicate any of these vessels or create your own shapes.

BROKEN VESSELS is a simple up and down arrangement of the chalice shapes. The break is a connecting line and is curvy cut before rectangling-up; it also implies a break by occurring across the blocks from one side of the piece to the other.

"Breaking" each block individually is much more difficult than rectangling-up, sewing the blocks together, and then making one continuous break (cut). I highly suggest making one cut for consistency in the curve.

RIGHT: BROKEN VESSELS, 33¼" x 45¼", made by the author, was inspired by part of Psalm 31:12: "I am like a broken vessel."

Instructions –
Broken Vessel Curvies

Begin with a grouping of fabrics and stack them to curvy cut.

Sew each group of 4 horizontal rectangles together.

Make 1 very gentle curvy cut across the sewn-together unit.

Use that cut as a guide for making the first cut into a larger piece of fabric that will become a slender insert.

Sew the first cut and insert together. This time, instead of beginning at the edge of the unit, begin in the middle. Use this as a general rule when sewing long stretches of a curve. You have a better chance of getting it to lie flat.

Make another curvy cut on the insert fabric with a nice, gentle curve. Do not make the lines equidistant but also don't make them too terribly slender.

Beginning in the middle, sew the remaining piece of the 4-unit rectangle to the slender fabric.

Spritz and press aggressively.

RIGHT: The author's quilt, RESTORED GOBLETS, 37½" x 23¾", used a group of the same design fabrics in a mini-dot. This did not give enough variety to the goblets, thus black, white, and other solids were added to give more boldness to the quiet piece. Instead of inserting a slender curvy shape, a cut was made across each goblet.

OPPOSITE: The blocks in A CHALICE BROKEN AND MENDED, 27" x 47½", were unused and left over, but when the pieces were broken with a curvy cut and put back together, the quilt was "mended." Give in folks, when the fabrics fight. Give in and let them have their own way.

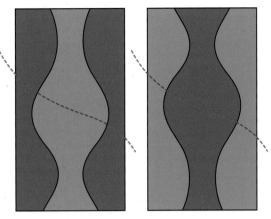

Fig. 2-12: Always turn one of the vessels upside down. The dotted line shows where the curvy cut will be. Note: 1 goblet will be shorter when sewn together.

Fig. 2-13: See how the bottom portion of the previous vessel has been placed on top of the next pair? This is your guide for the other 3 blocks.

Hints:
- Find the midpoint of the block by folding it in half.
- Match 2 top and bottom units as best you can.
- Sew from the middle to one end.
- Turn the unit to the other side (180 degrees).
- Sew from the middle to the end.

Instructions – 4 Vessel Shapes

There are 4 different shapes of vessels in RESTORED GOBLETS (page 29).

For each design, find 2 fabrics and create pairs of the same fabrics.

Take each pair, turn one upside-down and place it on top of the other in the pair (Fig. 2–12). *Do not mix one of this coloration with one of another. How do I know? I tried it and it looks horrid.*

Press together the upside-down pairs.

Make a gentle curvy cut through the 2 vessel blocks, one right-side up and the other upside down.

Take one of the pieces of the previous curvy cut and use it as a guide to make the same cut for the other 3 vessels (Fig. 2–13). By repeating the same cut you will have a continuous line throughout all 4 blocks. The same curvy cut gives an appearance of consistency to your finished piece.

Sew the new broken vessels together along the gentle curvy cuts by beginning the stitching in the middle of each vessel to help the block lie flat.

Do not be alarmed when you see that a strange phenomenon occurs when you sew the new pairs together. One pair is shorter than the other. This can make for an interesting off-set configuration of your piece.

You can see that the dominant design element is the gentle curvy sewn line that flows from one unit to the next (Fig. 2–14, page 31).

The only problem you may experience is that the units may not sew together perfectly without the addition of what I call "connectors."

If your piece does not need connectors, go ahead and sew them together without any. However, if yours asks for connectors, I suggest using a bold geometric print that works nicely. For mine, a black and ecru was a perfect choice (Fig. 2–15). I often rely on the non-colors of black and white (ecru is white, isn't it?) to complement a piece without calling attention to itself.

Now to sew the units together, you must first find a width for all units as well as two different lengths for the short and the long units.

For the width of *all* units, you must locate the vessel unit that has the *smallest* width increment. Rotary cut the widths of all units, using this increment.

For the length of the long units, locate the vessel unit that has the *smallest* length increment. Rotary cut the lengths of the long units using this increment.

For the length of the short units, locate the vessel unit that has the *smallest* length increment. Rotary cut the lengths of the short units using this increment.

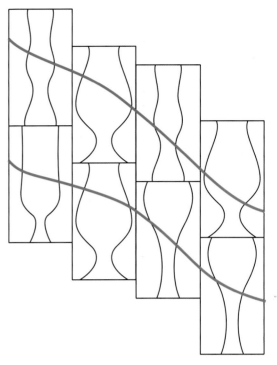

Fig. 2-14: The curvy cuts run through the piece, becoming the dominant design element.

BELOW: **Fig. 2-15:** RESTORED GOBLETS, detail, full quilt page 29. Connectors made in black and ecru.

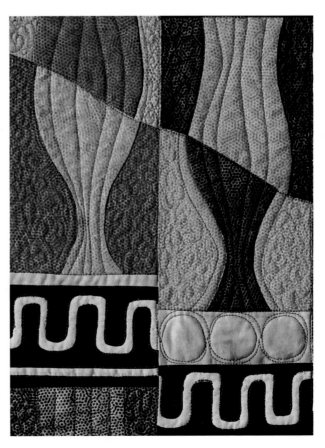

Hint: When I add connectors and/or fabrics as poppers, often this discovery, which is by accident, makes my quilts sing with joy, so I take no credit for it. It's a happening—a gut-reactive happening that occurs somewhere between the fabric stash and the design wall. It is when the eye has become a part of the hand and the hand has become part of the design being created. The hand serendipitously reaches for fabric(s) without thinking beyond placement onto the wall. "Reactive" is perhaps the best word to describe this happening.

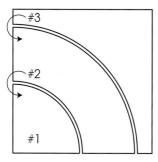

Fig. 2-16: Begin sewing these 3 units together by stitching the middle curvie (2) to the inner curvie (1). Sew the outer curvie (3) last. Before sewing, always arrange your block components in advance.

Sew the first 2 units together matching the curvy line but leave 1" open at the beginning and at the end of the seam. This will allow you to add connectors if you need them without ripping out the seam (a real timesaver).

Repeat by stitching the other pairs together in the same way. Add connectors to fill in between the units where necessary.

Circular Curvies

Circular curvies, sewn side-to-adjacent-side, are best used to either create broken circles or the 4 corners of a border (Fig. 2–16). Including them within the middle of other types of curvies certainly will work, but takes a bit of manipulation. Refer to Fig. 2–1c, page 18; the corners of the continuous curvy border need another type of curvy. This figure (Fig. 2–17) is a perfect example of circular curvies whether 2-color or 3-color.

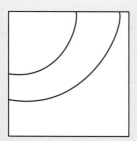 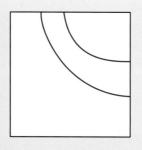 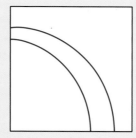 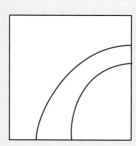

Fig. 2-17: For a configuration such as Jane Beaver's quilt, Going Round in Circles, page 33, rotary cut from one-side-to-its-adjacent-side. No matter on which side you begin or end your side-to-adjacent-side cut, you will always be able to create a broken circle. The name of her quilt is two-fold. Not only did she create a center grouping of broken circles, she also went around the entire quilt with a dynamic border created of side-to-opposite-side continuous curvies.

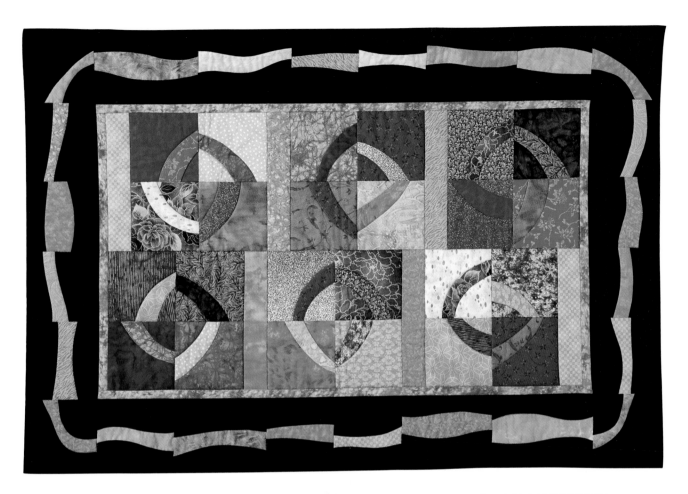

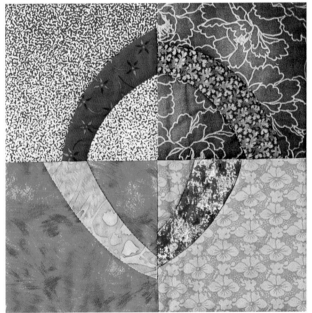

ABOVE: Jane Beaver of Ghent, West Virginia, created GOING ROUND IN CIRCLES, 42" x 28". This 2-colorway circular curvy quilt includes a green popper added to each block, creating an offset image.

RIGHT: GOING ROUND IN CIRCLES, detail

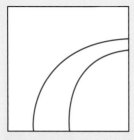

Fig. 2-18a: This gentle cut is side-to-adjacent-side.

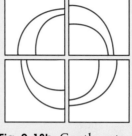

Fig. 2-18b: Gentle cuts create a well-executed broken circles design.

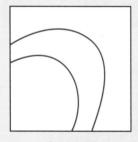

Fig. 2-18c: This is a flat cut.

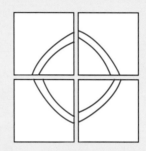

Fig. 2-18d: Flat cuts are, well, basically "flat"!

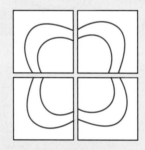

Fig. 2-18e: This is a sharp cut.

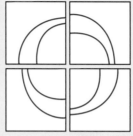

Fig. 2-18f: Sharp cuts create an interesting loopy-design formation that might be fun for florals.

If you have a minimum of 24 different circular curvies, you will be able to interchange all the blocks and thus attain more color permutations. If you plan to create a quilt similar to CENTRIFUGE, page 41, I suggest that you make a minimum of 24 to get a good color mix. More is much better.

As the only difference between circular curvies and continuous curvies is where you place your rotary cut (see page 11), the same instructions for selecting fabrics, making gentle cuts, rearranging the components, and sewing apply (Fig. 2–18a–f).

Corner Curvies

There are two types of corner curvies; both are useful. The side-to-one-corner curvy is best to take a viewer's eye across a quilt, connecting other blocks (Figs. 2–19 and 2–20, page 35); a corner-to-corner curvy is great when used in a stand-alone design.

For a meandering technique, a side-to-one-corner design may be used to travel across a quilt and to connect other designs. BALLET, page 35, incorporates this technique to create an aimlessly wandering effect in the top portion of the piece. By having the top portion deviate from the circular designs at the bottom, resolution of the top's meandering is given punctuation.

Should I execute the side-to-one-corner curvies sketched design in fabric, the colors would be clear and bold. With such a lively combination as a center, I might opt to settle it down with border(s) of blacks and whites. For my brightest quilts, black and white has become a wonderful stabilizing or calming device. Often I incorporate these two non-colors without thinking. It is a hand-reaching thing, done without giving any real thought to what I do. Allow yourself that freedom, too. Give your color-selecting brain a rest and let your fingers do the walking through your fabric stash.

Fig. 2-19: Four different configurations for side-to-one-corner curvies

LEFT: **Fig. 2-20:** See how using all side-to-one-corner curvies creates a webbing effect.

RIGHT: BALLET, 64" x 84", made by the author, uses a corner-to-one-side curvy shape to travel and connect, beginning at the top of the quilt and meandering in a dance-like movement. At the bottom, the "dancer" pirouettes in circles across the floor.

Fig. 2-21: There are 2 colors and 3 units for each corner-to-corner curvy block.

The second corner curvy is corner-to-corner. Just as its name implies, this block goes from opposite corner to opposite corner.

This design is a bit less staccato than the corner-to-one-side curvy. Both are best used as a single design and both types are ever so slightly more difficult to incorporate into a larger quilt than other curvy blocks, but are doable. When you need to travel from one block to another, this configuration is a good solution.

By using only 2 colors in each block, a Bow Tie look-alike design would be another easy and fast construction of corner-to-corner curvies (Fig. 2–21).

ABOVE: LOCAL COLOR, 37" x 37", made by Jean Mullenaux of Arundel, Maine, has a great optical illusion—a lovely grid appears to overlay a Four-Patch block quilt.

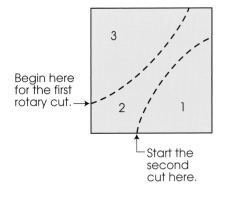

Hints:

⊙ No, the seams do not match. They cannot.

⊙ No, the curves do not match. They cannot.

⊙ Yes! The overall quilt may be seen as matching, although analysis will show an unmatched, staccato seam alignment.

When you make the corner-to-corner curvy cut, begin at one side and continue to the adjacent side. Remember to press the 4 fabrics into a stack before you cut in order to get a clean, consistent curve. Place your rotary cutter so that it is on the other side of the corner and make your cut to the adjacent side (Fig. 2–22).

Fig. 2-22: These 4 stacked fabrics are ready for a corner-to-corner curvy cut; only the top fabric shows. Begin sewing at the arrows, sewing #2 to #1, and then #3 to the 2-1 unit.

Combination Curvies

Another way you may sew the curvy blocks together is to place all of the two-color curvies into one quilt, no matter the type. You may give yourself permission to do that! It may require a bit more playing to find a design that you like, but it also may give you great joy when you find a satisfying arrangement.

When you combine several kinds of blocks together, often a more complex quilt is created. Look at CURVACEOUS SQUARES. Three kinds of curvies are used in this quilt: continuous, circular, and corner. Remember, it is important that you hold back one color range as your popper color to achieve uniformity and to pull your piece together as a unit (see "Popper Colors" on page 15).

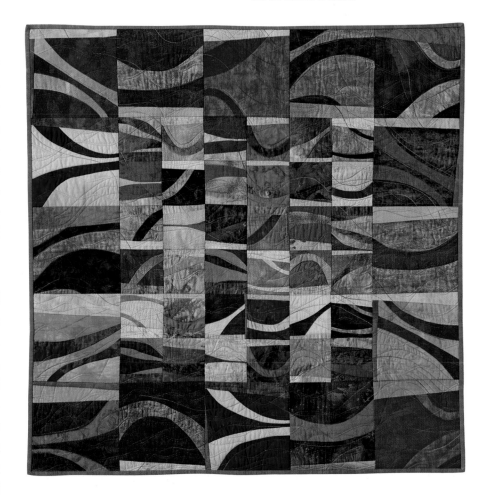

ABOVE: CURVACEOUS SQUARES, 39" x 39", made by the author, uses many shades from the green color family for poppers to achieve continuity.

ABOVE: THE MAINE LURE, 55" x 88", is a table runner created by Alice Hobbs Parsons of Belmont, Maine. It includes circular and continuous curvies and is owned by Ann and John Krumrein.

RIGHT: Detail of THE MAINE LURE, designed and made by Alice Hobbs Parsons for her friends, Ann and John Krumrein, as an attempt to pull them to Maine residency. It worked!

Crescent Curvies

Many crescent curvies, aka Drunkard's Path and other traditional block names, may be created to put some zing into traditional blocks (Figs. 2–23, 2–24, and 2–25).

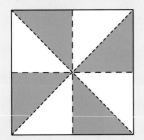 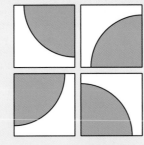

Fig. 2-23: Here a traditional Pinwheel block has been translated into a crescent pinwheel curvy block.

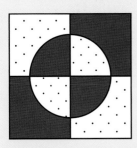 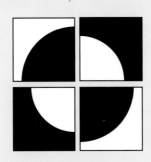

Fig. 2-24: By beginning with smaller squares, perhaps 4" x 4", and selecting many shades of black and white, an excellent, almost Polka Dot block design may be created.

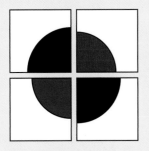 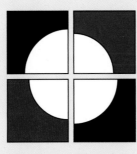

Fig. 2-25: This Polka Dot curvy block would make both a great quilt as well as a 4-block border. This time, use every shade of black and white, including navy, brown, gray, and dark green (as blacks) and cream, pale gray, off-white, stark white, etc., (as whites) and arrange the background colors as similar units.

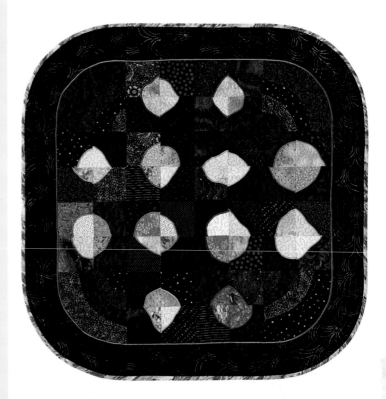

ABOVE: Peggy Ireland Elliott of Cumberland, Maine, took on the large Polka Dot curvy block as a challenge and created PLANETARY DISCOMFORT, 23¾" x 23¾".

BELOW: PLANETARY DISCOMFORT, detail.

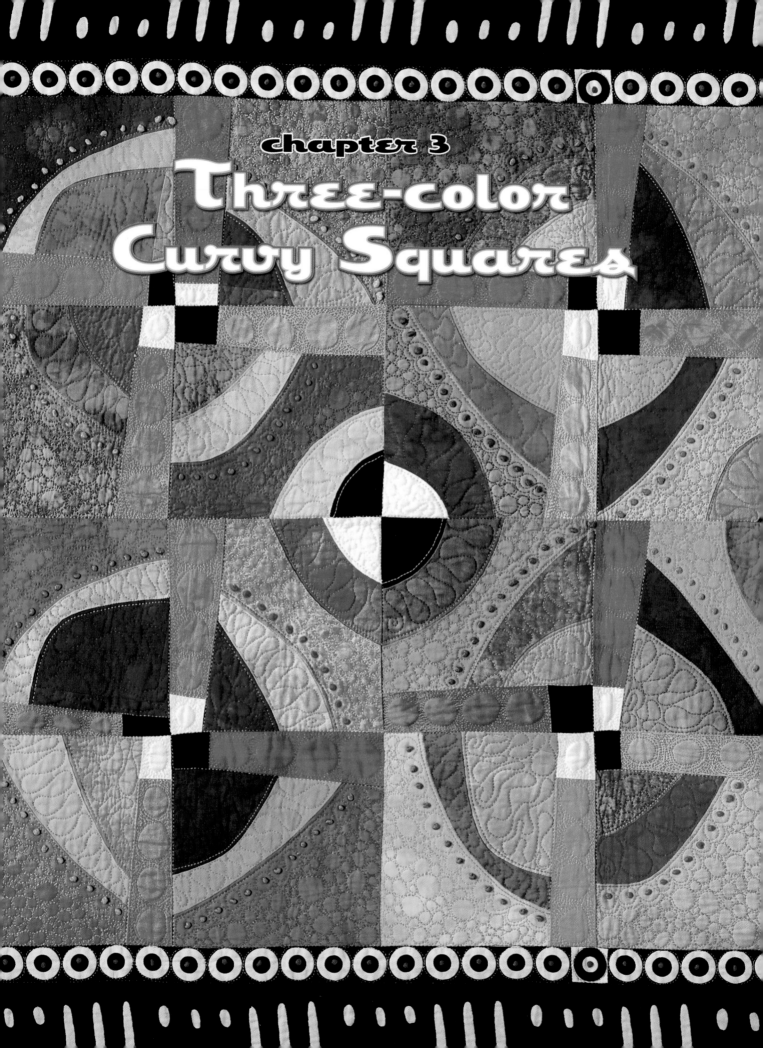

chapter 3

Three-color Curvy Squares

Laying out your designs with 3 different fabrics in each of the 4 blocks instead of only 2 fabrics in each offers even further design possibilities to explore. By interchanging the 4 fabrics, the same block becomes another design.

Compare my quilt CENTRIFUGE, below, with Jane Beaver's GOING ROUND IN CIRCLES (page 33). You will see that she used only 2 colors in her little blocks before sewing them into a broken circle unit, whereas mine has 3 colors in each one.

Both quilts are similar in that they are made up of 4 smaller little blocks arranged in broken circles. I want you to see that the same design may be created either way. Take a 2-colorway block, exchange one fabric in each of the 4 quadrants, and there you have it—a 3-color curvy block.

A few 3-color curvy blocks have as their basis an adaptation of a traditional block. Use the Turnstile block to see how the block can be made into curves although the lines were straight in the original design.

ABOVE: CENTRIFUGE, 49½" x 36¼", made by the author, has 3-color broken circle curvies.

OPPOSITE: CENTRIFUGE, detail

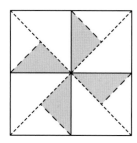 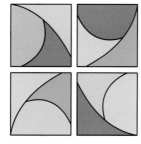

Fig. 3–1: When finished, the curvy Rotating Turnstile block looks like children's fun rotating windmills on a stick.

Rotating Turnstile Curvies

Curvy rotations must be created in a slightly different way from other 3-fabric combinations (Fig. 3–1). Instead of rotary cutting all of your curvy cuts at the same time, make each of the cuts one at a time and then stitch 2 cuts together. Begin with the longest cut. Because of the extraordinarily strong curvy lines and shape of this block, you need more leeway to change the size of the block (square) as you go along. Don't wait until all the seams are sewn together.

Instructions – Rotating Turnstile Curvies

The process is cut, sew, press; then cut, sew, press. With that rhythm in mind…

Fig. 3–2: Make the longest curvy cut similar to this broken line.

After making the first cut for the longest curve, rearrange the colors and sew and press the 2 components together in the same way described in Chapter 2 (Fig. 3–2).

After stitching the pieces back together, stack the 4 blocks by aligning the corners and pressing them to make it easier to cut through 4 seamed layers.

If you have any extra fabric sticking out from the blocks, rotary cut that away but don't bother to square them up.

Fig. 3–3: Use the broken line as a guide for the shorter curve.

Make the second curvy cut in a similar way: rearrange the colors, sew, and press (Fig. 3–3).

WAIT to square up the blocks until after you have made all the blocks you need for your quilt. REPEAT: WAIT. I mean it. Really. Wait.

If you go ahead and square up your blocks before you have created enough for a finished top, you may find that a block or two will be smaller than all the rest. Such a problem often makes for a bit of a creative challenge. However, when that occurs, the outcome sometimes gives your quilt more dynamic visual interest and a design opportunity. I suggest adding fabric(s) of another but similar shade to the smaller culprit.

ABOVE RIGHT: LIFE IS A WHIRL, detail

RIGHT: Sally K. Field of Hampden, Maine, created LIFE IS A WHIRL, 37" x 37". It is an excellent example of a Rotating Turnstile curvy block. The detail photo clearly shows her choice of coloring each turnstile with a similar shade.

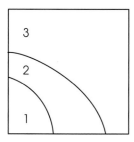

Fig. 3–4: Here is a sketch of your block with each piece numbered. Color swaths are determined by pieces 1 and 3.

Curvy Pathways

Curvy Pathways are traditionally called Drunkard's Path, Wanderer's Path, Oregon Trail, Boston Trail, or Solomon's Puzzle. This particular curvy arrangement requires a manipulation of colors (Fig. 3–4). Each red is actually a shade of orange, fuchsia, hot pink, or reddish-orange. In the same way, each lime green is every shade of lime you can find, as is the blue-purple and the yellow. It goes without saying at this point that the more shades and values you can insert within a colorway, the more exceptional the flow of color (Fig. 3–5).

Hints: Unless you jumped in and started reading this chapter first, I think you understand the steps for rotary cutting, ⅛" seam allowance stitching, water spritzing, and aggressive pressing. Remember that the same methods are used throughout every type of curvy. If you need a review, look at pages 9–12. Sometimes it helps to give a return look, especially if it has been a while since you read about curvy techniques.

Fig. 3–5: Movement across a quilt is created when you use curvy pathways in a 3-color combination.

ABOVE: CURVY PATHWAYS, 38" x 30", was made by the author. Look at the colors of piece 1 and piece 3. I manipulated these two to form diagonal swaths. Buttons and beads added further emphasis to the yellow and red color swaths.

RIGHT: THE TIDE IS HIRE, 51" x 51", was made by Sarah Ann Smith of Camden, Maine. Her quilt is heavily quilted with many threads and is hand beaded. See how the final quilt has her own stamp of originality to it as she turns the blocks on point instead of straight. It is in the collection of the International Quilt Festival, Houston, Texas; used by permission of Karey Bresenhan.

LEFT: Kate Elliott of Casselberry, Florida, made CLASS CLOWN, 43" x 41", which flows with 3 fabrics (large, bold geometrics and prints) in each block. Instead of a quarter circle, Kate played with double-cut, continuous curvies side-to-opposite side.

BELOW: PENOBSCOT WAVES, 34" x 20", made by Ruth Lind, Stockton Springs, Maine, uses the same blocks, rearranged to depict waves lapping the coastline.

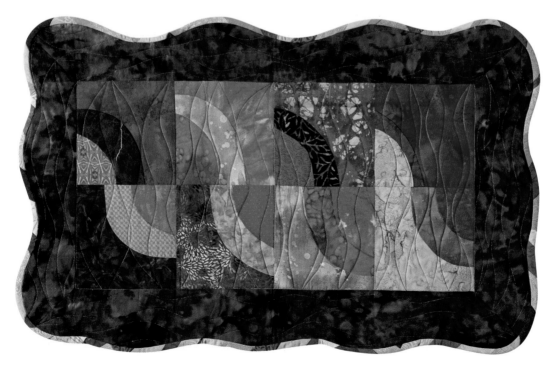

RIGHT: WAVES OF A WARRIOR, 59" x 71", made by Ruth Lind of Stockton Springs, Maine, presents undulating color bands. Since Ruth lives near and views the ocean daily, her interpretation is about the dramatic waves striking the coast of Maine.

BELOW: Pat Hammeke of Marshfield, Wisconsin, squared up her blocks and arranged her Curvy Pathways in a more traditional manner. FABULOUS CURVES WITH LITTLE WORK, 32½" x 21½", is on a diagonal with the spaces between the inset curves giving the appearance of similar fabrics. How about this quilt's name? Didn't I tell you it is an easy technique?

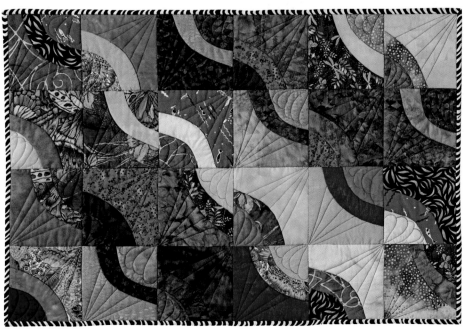

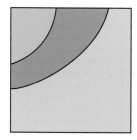

Fig. 3–6: In about 3 hours there were over 100 of these broken circle calico curvies stacked on my cutting board and I was without a clue as to what to do with them. Long story short, the end result is that I am very fond of this one little quilt.

Calico Capers

Shhh-hhhhh, because I'm about to share a secret with you. My forté is having the coloring sense of a first grader, meaning a colorist with bold and energetic bright colors. However, there is a secret love for calicoes within this otherwise "bright" (colored) brain. (Note: I did *not* say RIGHT brain.)

Here's why I share that…in the first draft of this book, my intention was to include a whole chapter of calico capers, and yes, every single one was to be made of wonderful, soothing, and many-printed calicoes. So-o-o-o-o, one Saturday morning I sat down to make curvy-calico blocks in the broken circle design (Fig. 3–6).

Did I make other little calico quilts, you ask? Well, yes, and those weren't so great and are shelved quite nicely, thank you very much. Even the blocks were ignored until Peggy Ireland Elliot took the sad little box of my not-so-loved curvy-calico critters home with her to see if she could make anything at all of them (FLEUR-DE-LESS, page 49).

LEFT: CALICO CAPERS, 28¼" x 28¼", made by the author, has buttons, beads, and embroidery threads and was machine appliquéd. It was machine quilted by Joan Herrick, who, as we fondly tease, "taught Dianne everything she knows about quilting!"

RIGHT: Peggy Ireland Elliott of Cumberland, Maine, had fun naming her wonderful 18" x 18" calico-caper curvy quilt— FLEUR-DE-LESS. Don't you love it? Her design sense is excellent, as is her exquisitely elegant beading.

Circular Curvies with Windmills

I'm often asked how a design comes about. Nearly always a new design is the result of having to "make" something happen, of having to work out a potential disaster.

For example, CENTRIFUGE (pages 40–41) "happened" because I am lazy. You see I did not want to square up the blocks thereby making them much smaller. Instead, I wanted to keep the blocks closer to the size with which I began—6" x 6". To do that, something needed to be added somewhere to the blocks to increase their size.

Wedges were added. I liked them. It looked pretty good. Blocks were placed on the design wall, and, well, the rest is history.

For a wallhanging such as this one, begin with 24 squares of fabrics. One caveat, however: *you must* always begin to stitch your units together on the left-hand side (see Fig. 1–11b on page 14). This is especially important to successfully put a quilt together in the manner of CENTRIFUGE. If you change midstream and sew from the top, bottom, or right-hand side, you will have differing rotations and that does not work.

After all the blocks are stitched together, add the wedges to make strong moving windmills. Whatever number of fabrics with which you begin will be the number of blocks when sewn together, e.g., your selected 24 fabrics will yield 24 little blocks. Those 24 little blocks will yield 6 circular curvies with windmills.

To see how that is done, look at Laura Christensen's design wall (Fig. 3–7). Some of her blocks have been sewn together, but that is only after she completely designed her 6 blocks. The bottom 3 are not squared up yet. Here you can see that these 24 small blocks (quadrants of a circle) are combined into 6 curvy circles and become major design elements when sewn together.

LEFT: Fig. 3–7: Laura Christensen of Bardstown, Kentucky, is shown with her 24 circular-curvies-with-windmills blocks at the Kentucky Heritage Quilt Society's 2004 Design Seminar.

Instructions – Circular Curvies with Windmills

Select 6 sets of 4 color-family fabrics. For the best combinations in a finished quilt, each of the 24 fabrics should be unique. Create 24 squares cutting them all the same size anywhere from 6" to 7". Example colorways would be 6 greens, 6 blues, 6 yellows, and 6 purples.

From this grouping, select one fabric from each of the 4 different color families. Stack and then press them together for ease in rotary curvy cutting.

Make circular curvies (side-to-*adjacent*-side cuts; see pages 32–34). Create broken circles, but instead of making the finished block with only 2 colors, use 3 colors in each block. When you create 4 blocks using 3 colors in each, you have many more options to colorize and give contrasts that work nicely.

Sew the block by stringing the components together with a ⅛" seam allowance.

Repeat until you have rotary cut, pressed, and sewn all 24 blocks. Let's call these "quadrant" blocks because they will be sewn together as a 4-block unit soon.

I suggest that a good way to arrange your assorted quadrant blocks on your design wall is to find background colors that are similar. By background, I mean the largest circular area (Fig. 3–8, page 51).

Squaring up the block entails a bit of size-searching after you have arranged the blocks in the design or combination you like best.

Keeping the blocks in the design arrangement that you like the most, locate the block that has the *smallest increment* on the non-ragged side of your stitched block. Let's call that increment the "limiter," because you are limited to block size by the non-ragged side that has the smallest increment (Fig.3–9, page 51).

Select a popper color, which will be the rotating windmill blade. Notice that no true reds were used in my quadrant blocks for CENTRIFUGE (pages 40–41). Reds were withheld from the mix in order to use them as a popper color. I define "red" as orange, hot pink, lilac, fire engine, apple red, fuchsia, and raspberry to get an array of colorations (Fig. 3–10).

Create rectangles from the popper fabrics approximately 3" wide with a length about 2" longer than your quadrant block (Fig. 3–11). Arrange them around the sewn quadrant blocks, keeping your design intact.

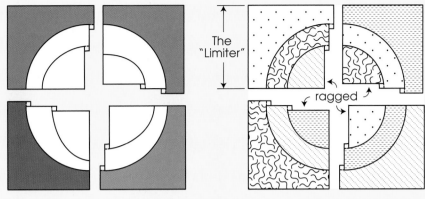

Fig. 3–8: These 4 quadrant blocks have similar lavender (purple) backgrounds.

Fig. 3–9: These 4 blocks are arranged in a circular design with 1 inner side ragged and 1 non-ragged. The outside smallest "limiter" will determine the length x width of all of the quadrant blocks.

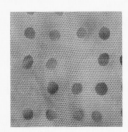
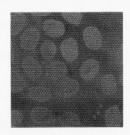
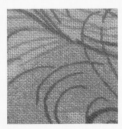

Fig. 3–10: Use a wide array of colorations for your popper. These are just a few reds. For active movement, use different shades of your popper color for each blade.

Find several shades of black and white fabrics. Cut these into 3" squares. Place these on the arrangement of your circular design, and then recut them as little wedges.

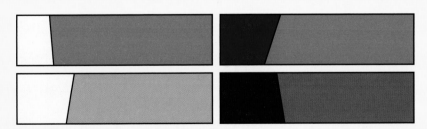

Fig. 3–11: These 4 rectangles 3" wide are ready to be sewn onto the ragged sides of the quadrant blocks.

Hints: True solids work best because of the clarity they offer.

Also, using ranges of colors adds zing. In Centrifuge (see pages 40–41), I used off-white, true white, beige-white, and stark white for "white." For "black" I used black-brown, purple-black, blue-black, navy, midnight black, and even dark gray. Using all of these colors makes for a more interesting quilt. Your eye sees "black" and "white," but close examination reveals the use of other shades. How fun is that?

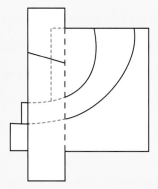

Fig. 3–12: The dotted line indicates where you should sew the popper rectangles. The red dotted line will help you pretend you have x-ray vision to view the ragged side.

In different wedge-shapes and with no extremely sharp angles, sew the blacks and whites onto the popper fabrics.

Rotary cut a straight edge off the ragged sides, addressing each quadrant block *one at a time* to keep from mixing them up and to keep your intended design intact. Cut a gentle angle, not a sharp one. Make the cut so that the blade will be smaller in the center and increase in size as it goes outward toward the edge.

Sew the rectangles onto the quadrant blocks (Fig. 3–12).

Using a see-through 12" square ruler, square up the quadrant blocks to whatever increment you found to be the limiter, creating wedge-shaped windmill blades at the same time. When you square-up the blocks, it is helpful to orient each of them in the same direction (Fig. 3–13). Your newly acquired x-ray vision helps, too.

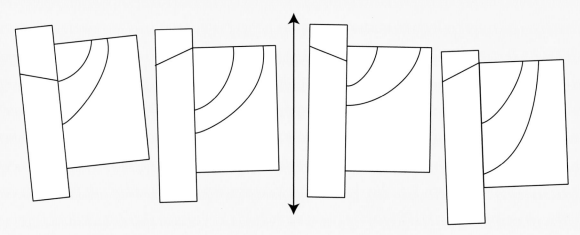

Fig. 3–13: For rotary cutting, orient each of your quadrant blocks in the same direction on the rotary mat.

Sew the 4 quadrants together (Fig. 3–14), taking care to match the center seams—just like normal quiltmakers do! Often, to get a perfect match without pinning, I begin in the middle and sew to the exterior of one side. Then, I turn the block over to begin again in the middle and sew to the exterior of the other side.

Again, look at CENTRIFUGE (pages 40–41) with its revolving windmill blades. Notice that the backgrounds of each quadrant were consolidated into groupings of blues, greens, yellows, etc. Well, yes, I know that orange isn't yellow, but it works!

If a color background refuses to work for you, it is an easy task to use the rotary cutter to remove the offensive background and add another. Underneath the quadrant, have a square block (the size being that of the original squares) in a color that works. Use the curvy-cutting method of cutting both at once (see pages 22–24). Add the new color and you are off and running.

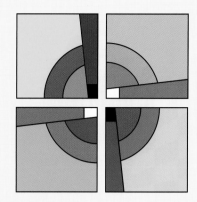

Fig. 3–14: The quadrant blocks are squared up and ready to be sewn together.

This is me with CENTRIFUGE!

RIGHT: Janet Houts of Bellevue, Idaho, created a vertical wallhanging. It is 10" x 31" and entitled FRISBEE FLING. Her slender blades in blue are a great complement to the orange broken circle quadrants. Janet also gave the method a perfectly wonderful name—"courageous curves!"

Three-color Curvy Squares

With the same exact procedure, a lovely little quilt may be created.

ABOVE: My quilt, CURVY SUNBLAZE, 15¾" x 15¾", also on the cover, has 4 shades of pale lilac (poppers) and 4 shades for the yellow centers as it whirls around. It is accessorized with glass bugle beads for a little bling, dotty-beads, and buttons. The border fabric dictated the quilting as well as the beading.

3-Color Curvy Quilts Gallery

Among other outstanding quilts with the 3-colorway side-to-adjacent-side curvy technique was one created by Karin Peirce of Belmont, Maine. Notice that the borders are also 3-colorway blocks, but see how Karin created a fanciful open-floral limb on the right-hand side from which the bird pecks. Karin's trick is that she usually works by hand; very little is created by machine. Yes, she hand pieced her fun quilt and decorated it with many, many embroidery stitches.

LEFT: Folkloric in nature, Karin Peirce's SHADY GARDEN, 27¼" x 44½", uses 3-colorway curvy blocks as a backdrop for birds, flowers, and leaves in an imaginary sanctuary.

BELOW: Jeanne-Marie Robinson of Northport, Maine, used her Pinwheel blocks to surround a bowl full of veggies appliquéd on a backdrop of printed black-and-white fabric. This is ORANGE AID, 53½" x 41". See how the border transitions from beautiful muted colors to the neutral of black-and-white.

RIGHT: CROP CIRCLES, 20¼" x 20¼", was made by Peggy Ireland Elliott of Cumberland, Maine. It glows with blues and turquoises combined with yellows and oranges.

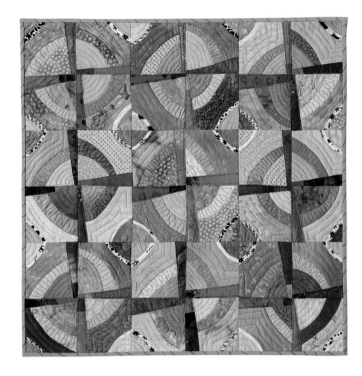

It is my pleasure to end this chapter with a quilt that may be one of my favorites. Janet Myers' WHIRLYGIGS has combined many of the *Quilters Playtime* (AQS, 2004) games such as Hopscotch, Checker-Border, and Pin the Tail on the Donkey with her vivacious curvy blocks. It is my joy to show this quilt. I probably could never say enough good things about it. Thank you to Janet for sharing it with us all.

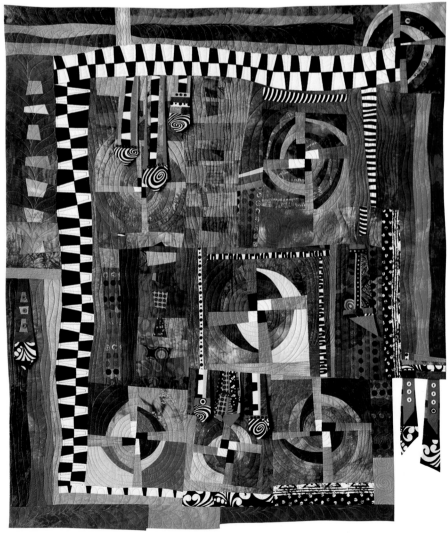

RIGHT: WHIRLYGIGS, 49" x 56", by Janet Myers of Flandreau, South Dakota, is a quilt that has my heart singing.

chapter 4
Curvy Rectangles

Curvy Rectangles

Since making all of those quilts from 6" to 7" curvy squares turned out to be so much fun, it seemed worth the effort to work with rectangles to see what might occur. A chance discovery blessed me once more.

Instead of making curves to create blocks, the difference is to begin with larger rectangles. The method creates very lovely wallhangings that might be cut, sewn together, and ready to sandwich and quilt in just over 3 hours. This method is especially good if you have a wall that might use a horizontal piece.

This wallhanging project lends itself to soft, more fluid fabrics without a lot of strong contrasting prints or colors. I suggest hand-dyed fabrics or similar commercial textiles in related colors rather than four bold, powerfully differing colorations (such as a true red, a cadet blue and a lemon yellow with an apple green).

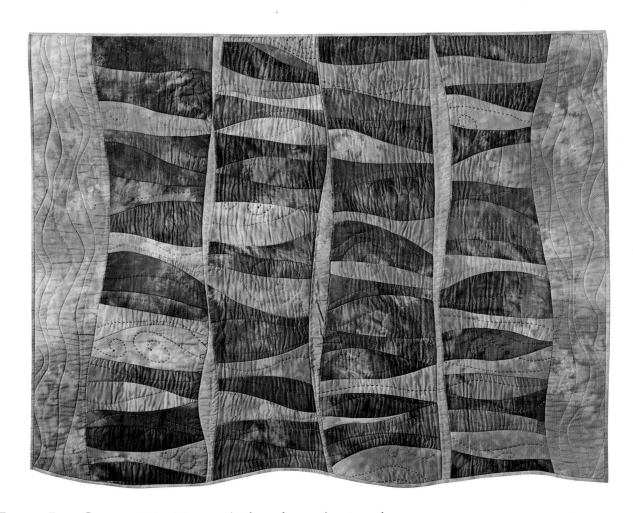

ABOVE: RAIN CLOUDS, 47" x 47", was the first of several rectangular quilts I made using this technique. Six strands of embroidery floss were used to create large-stitch quilting in pale colors of yellow, peach, lavender, blue, lime, and turquoise. The stitches added dimension to the soft fabric shades.

OPPOSITE: RAIN CLOUDS, detail

Fig. 4–1: These 4 fabrics are stacked for rotary cutting; only the top fabric shows.

Fig. 4–2: Create a 3-panel layout and use the extra 4th panel as needed.

Fig. 4–3: Sew unit #2 to unit #1; then unit #3 to the 2-1 unit. Continue in this way working from bottom to top.

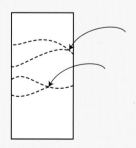

Fig. 4–4: An interior curvy should be sewn beginning in the interior, not at the edge.

Instructions – Curvy Rectangles

To begin, select 3 or 4 vertical panels of fabrics. If you have a wall in mind for placement of a piece such as this, measure the space that might work. Let's say that an optimal size of the piece would be 18" long. Next, figure out approximately how wide the piece should be in its final form. Let's say that would be 36" wide. Divide that by 3 and you get 12" wide. However, by using 4 panels that are 12" x 18", you have the ability to give the piece more diversity by substituting pieces from the 4th panel into the 3-panel layout. Stay with me. Or see figure 4-2.

If you want a small wallhanging, create each rectangle approximately 6" wide x 10" long. For a larger one, create each rectangle as wide and as long as you wish. The beauty of this technique is that it may be easily adapted in size by increasing or decreasing the rectangles' dimensions.

Make a series of horizontal curvy-cuts (gentle, of course) across the width of the entire stack of 4 rectangles (Fig. 4–1).

One by one, place the separate pieces into 3 vertical arrangements as shown. Note that the 4th fabric is the extra panel that may be inserted at whim whenever and wherever needed (Fig. 4–2).

Arrange and rearrange the curvy-cut fabrics until you are pleased with the visual effect of the 3 panels. If needed, use the 4th fabric as an accent color or print to make your curvy-transitions work. Sometimes you may actually end up with 4 complete panels instead of 3 and will be able to use all of them. That's a bonus that may or may not occur, depending on your arrangement and your fabric selections.

Begin sewing the pieces on the left-hand side. Start at the bottom of the design layout, sewing piece #2 to piece #1 (Fig. 4–3). This keeps you from knocking the fabric layout off the table as you sew and keeps your design intact. Continue sewing upward toward the top/last piece until all of the curvy-units are sewn into place (Fig. 4–4).

Before you think about sewing your 3 panels together, just for the fun of it, flip one or more of the panels upside-down. Do you like the new arrangement of the 3 panels? If so, keep them in that order. Also, move the panels to different locations. Sometimes more serendipity occurs if you let it happen.

Curly Curvies

Ready to sew each panel together? The next step is learning how to insert curly curvies between each panel. Remember to use ⅛" seams when sewing curvies.

Curly curvies are wonderful for inserting between rectangles. These accentuate your curves vertically and act as connectors between each horizontal panel. Select colors that do not take away from your major design (Fig. 4–5).

BELOW: **Fig. 4–5**: The sketch and quilt, BLUE CLOUDS, 31" x 43½", were made by the author. Imagine how this soft palette of gentle blues would be completely upset if the bright red from the sketch had been used. Six-strand embroidery floss was used to fasten the buttons onto the quilt in linear curvy rows. This embellishment echoed the movement created by the inset curly curvies. Glossy beads were also fastened into place with long stitches.

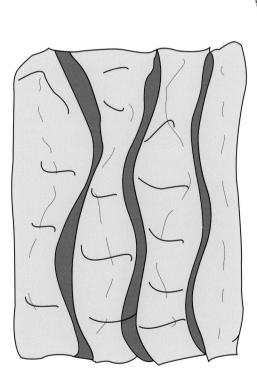

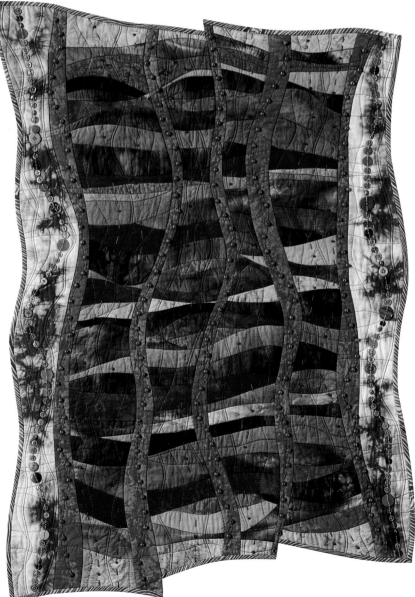

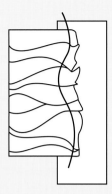

Fig. 4–6: Create a gentle curly curvy cut through 2 fabrics— the sewn panel and the fabric underneath it. The bottom fabric will become the inserted vertical curly-curvy accent.

Instructions – Curly Curvies

To create a curly curvy, place a larger piece of fabric behind the sewn-together panel. This fabric hangs well below the horizontally sewn-together unit. Having such extra fabric at the bottom is important with this method because the seam, when stitched without any templates, moves downward onto this fabric and you do not want to run out at the bottom (Fig. 4–6).

Stitch together the first panel with the accent vertical curly curvy leaving all of the accent fabric intact—do not cut it off. The general rule is to keep this curvy larger than you need until you have something onto which to sew.

Place the second panel on the accent fabric and make another curly curvy with your rotary cutter. Sew together those 2 units.

Repeat this process until all of the panels and curly curvies are in place.

Add a border on the right and on the left.

Hint: Envision how you would like a curve to be cut. Sometimes a little practice making gentle long cuts *without the blade open* is helpful. When you feel comfortable with the way the gentle curve looks in your mind, rotary curvy cut through both the sewn-together panel and the fabric underneath it. Take care to always cut through 2 fabrics with your gentle curves. Remember: a simple curve is more appealing than one with lots of motion.

Curvy Rectangle Quilts Gallery

ABOVE: Joyce Grande of Cape Coral, Florida, created a layering effect composed of several horizontal rectangular curved units to make a single backdrop. JUNGLE FEVER, approximately 38" x 36", shows how she overlapped several little curvy quilts to make an exciting backdrop to showcase her jungle leaf motif. The many curvy hanging doo-dads are bead embellished, and Joyce's leaves are cutouts enhanced with beads and found things.

Two California quiltmakers, Kristen E. Eilers of LeMoore and Charlotte Rogers of Hanford, took the idea of rectangular curves and ran with it. It is a joy when these simple beginnings turn into more excellent designs. Look at Kristen's first interpretation; she rotated a foursome around a central block of lime green.

ABOVE AND RIGHT: Compare the above work-in-progress with Kristen's finished quilt, RANDOM RIVER DIVIDES SYMMETRY, 38¾" x 38¾". She made a 45-degree turn of the rotating blocks on point and added a vertical lime curly curvy with triangular borders.

LEFT: This quilt, RECTANGULAR CURVIES, 25¾" x 13½", was created in the exact same way as BLUE CLOUDS (page 61). However, I inserted another curly curve down the center of the middle panel. Another difference is that the quilt was turned 90-degrees to make it a vertical wallhanging. I used this little piece to practice my machine quilting until there was not one space left to quilt any further. Notice that the warm pink curly curvies are in the same color family as the top and bottom reddish-pink-plum borders. Having this kind of color continuity makes a piece come together in its final form.

ABOVE: Charlotte Rogers, of Hanford, California, designed a favorite piece using the rectangles as a beginning. Her jagged edges are right down my design alley. I recall her saying it took great discipline to cut into a piece of Ricky Tims' wonderful hand-dyed fabric. Her finished piece, CANYON COUNTRY, 32" x 31", was worth it, especially with the addition of hanging threads, silk ribbons, and beads.

LEFT: CANYON COUNTRY, detail

chapter 5
Curvy Botanicals

ince both quilting and gardening are high on my list of passions, it is only appropriate that botanicals would enter this curvy book's picture. This is one of the easiest designs to adapt into either a square or rectangular design, depending on whether your leaf is fat like a philodendron (square) or linear like a palm (rectangle) or somewhere in between, like an imaginary leaf.

Normally when I create a quilt, it goes against my grain to create anything that resembles a real object. Instead, I take that reality and create a simulation of it with nothing but my imagination to fall back upon. However, leaf designs do appeal to me with my love of gardening; thus, it seemed a natural to create fairly realistic leaves using the curvy method.

OPPOSITE: LEAVES FOR HEALING, detail, full quilt pages 68–69

BELOW: CONNECT THE DOTS, 29" x 36", is an interpretation of the sketch in Fig. 5–1. It was created by Susanne Rivers of Searsport, Maine. She opted to add 3-D circle dots and to create her quilt horizontally.

Skinny Imaginary Leaves from Squares and Rectangles

I offer this design—2 sizes of skinny leaves (Fig. 5–1). The fabric requirement is that you have 8 rectangles and 8 squares. When sewn together and squared up, the completed quilt top will have 16 blocks.

Fig. 5–1: This design is made up of 2 sizes of leaves sewn together in an alternating pattern to give a staccato effect for excellent movement. The dotted lines show how additional blocks would look. If manipulated, slender flower petals emerge.

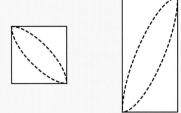

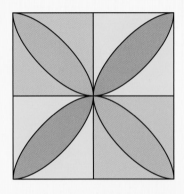

Fig. 5–2: Stack 4 pieces of fabric in preparation for making shapes of curvy cuts similar to these. Repeat for the next 4 fabrics.

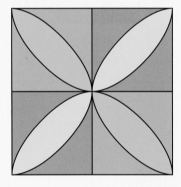

Fig. 5–3: Here is a flower with 4 petals arranged of the same Leaf blocks.

Instructions – Skinny Leaves

Select 8 fabrics and cut them into eight 6" squares. Select another 8 fabrics and cut those into eight 6" x 12" rectangles (Fig. 5–2).

In sets of 4 (instead of the entire 8 squares or rectangles), make curvy cuts. Make each set of 4 with a different cut to offer variety in the finished blocks.

Sew the blocks together, lifting and separating and pulling and pushing the components (see page 13 for these techniques).

Press aggressively toward the leaf portion (center) of the block.

Square up the blocks, including making true rectangles out of the larger rectangular leaf designs. Take care to keep as much of each leaf point as possible.

FYI: You may need to add a wedge or two here and there to the blocks to complete the finished design.

Just for the fun of it and before you sew the squares and rectangles together, try this: rearrange those same squares (Fig. 5–3). Do you like the new design better?

Imaginary Leaf Designs

There is so much that can be imagined using the curvy methods, I cannot wait to see what you create out of your own fantasies! Some of my sketched designs are influenced by real botanical things, but when interpreted this way end up being playful abstractions of reality (Figs. 5–4 and 5–5).

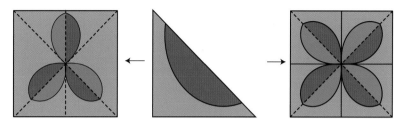

Fig. 5–4: The 3-leaf clover and 4-leaf clover shapes begin with a series of triangles rather than rectangles or squares. For this design, I suggest you begin stitching in the middle of the design instead of at the edge.

BELOW: LEAVES FOR HEALING, 36¼" x 13½", made by the author, called for interchanging the fabrics, which is always fun to do. Instead of full leaves, each mini-block has only a portion of a full leaf. There are 2 different leaf designs and each has a mirror image, which means 2 fabrics in each set of 4 must be turned upside-down.

Fig. 5–5: By making a couple of small changes to the triangle, a dogwood flower configuration may be created. Make one curvy cut beginning on a straight edge and ending on the diagonal, but change the soft curve to a pointy end. Use both the right side and the wrong side of fabrics to achieve 2 triangle petals. This sketch is a special memory from my home state of Tennessee, when in springtime the dogwood trees array the woods with white and pink blossoms.

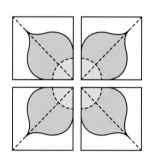

What about combining the 3-color curvy (see Chapter 3) with these for curvy botanicals? Instead of curves that flow across the rectangular panels, why not make these a series of leaf shapes from small to large and skinny to wide? The panels would simply undulate with movement! See figure 5–6 on page 70.

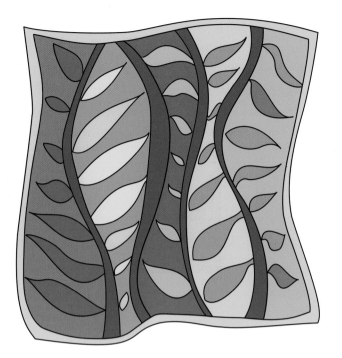

Fig. 5–6: First, cut curvies that look like leaves. Second, address each vertical cut individually to prevent wasting too much fabric.

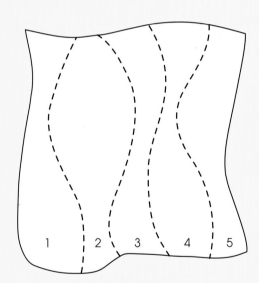

Fig. 5–7: Using muslin, rotary cut a pattern of the 5 vertical panels. Number them.

Instructions – Imaginary Leaves

Find 7 fabrics—5 for the verticals with leaves, 1 for the slender curved inserts, and a fabric you really could care less about, a throwaway fabric such as inexpensive muslin. This last fabric will be used as a pattern for the quilt top only. If you duplicate the sketch in figure 5–7, select 1 light, 1 medium-light, and 3 mediums plus 1 dark for the slender inserts. Set these aside.

It is easiest if you opt to make all the leaves the same color. If so, then choose 2 fabrics for each vertical panel, because you will spritz, then iron the 2 together before you cut your leaves. However, should you wish to make each leaf a different color, why not use your scraps, inserting different colors underneath the background panel? That makes great use of your scraps as well as gives diversity to your quilt.

Keep in mind that the finished piece will be smaller after it is stitched together than the increments with which you begin.

Rotary cut your throwaway pattern fabric (muslin) to a length and width just a bit larger than the approximate size of the finished top. Do not make any cuts for the slender inserts. Those will fall into place very naturally; you'll see.

Use each pattern to make a vertical of its corresponding selected fabric. However, if your leaves are to be only one color, press the pattern on top of 2 ironed-together fabrics and rotary cut both panels.

Place the panels onto a design wall to be sure you like the color arrangement; remember that there will be slender leaf inserts added later. Make leaf color changes now.

For a same-color leaf arrangement, take both units of panel #1 and make the leaf-shaped curvies. These cuts should be shapely cuts, but not too deeply shaped. However, give them nice, full figures. For a multi-color leaf arrangement, place the different fabrics underneath unit #1, then make each cut slowly and individually, also cutting shapely figures.

After you have cut panel #1 with leaves, place all the units on your design wall for assessing.

Repeat this same process of cutting, then placing on the design wall for the remaining 4 panels. Assess before you sew.

If you feel that more leaf colors are needed, fussy-cut and replace some leaves. Hand-dyed fabrics or commercial fabrics with multiple shadings offer a wonderful array of colors so that the panels are not so "stuffy-matched" in colorations.

Sew together each panel. Make sure to spritz and press aggressively before proceeding to add the slender inserts.

Review your chosen dark fabric for the slender inserts. Does it still work now that the panels are sewn together? If so, insert them, using the same curvy cut as unit #1's right-hand curve. Since the unit will be out of whack from how it began, place the muslin pattern on top of both the sewn-together leafy panel and the insert fabric. Use the pattern and rotary cut.

In order to vary the width and curvy shape of the slender insert, take the pattern for panel #2 and move it back and forth to find a nice shape. It is a matter of manipulating the pattern; it will be an illusion that the cut is not the same as the left-hand edge of panel #2. Try it.

Repeat for all inserts and VOILA! There you have it—an imaginary leaf wallhanging.

Fig. 5–8: How about another design? This time use only 4 panels and create a horizontal design, but move it 90 degrees left or right for placement of pieces and for stitchery purposes. Or, create another design with only 3 panels that could be made smaller and more quickly than the other two.

Imaginary Leaves Quilts Gallery

LEFT: Instead of vertical panels, Peggy Ireland Elliott of Cumberland, Maine, turned her design into a graceful horizontal quilt. BRANCHING MOONLIGHT, 21" x 21", was created in royal blue, purple, and muted grays. The leaves look like the moon has touched them.

RIGHT: DANCING LEAVES, 33" x 26", made by Susanne Rivers of Searsport, Maine, delights the senses with fun polka dots. Sharp lime leaves with a variety of red backgrounds are accented with slender black verticals.

Large-leaf Philodendron

If you like philodendron leaves, it's easy to create these imagined shapes using only 4 fabrics cut into 6" x 9" rectangles. These are fat little squatty things and are excitingly beautiful when backed with a fusible such as Wonder-Under and adhered onto one piece of background fabric (Fig. 5–9). An array of these imaginary curvy-cut leaves is fun to create because of the many, many possible colorations. You are not limited by reality. You have permission to use colorations that may never-ever be in a leaf. How fun is that?

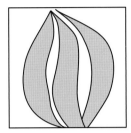  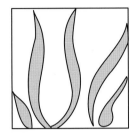

LEFT: **Fig. 5–9:** Another type of leaf is a fat horizontal or vertical curvy that may have more than one insert. This fanciful leaf resembles a large-leaf philodendron. Several of these would make a lovely backdrop. This design could also be developed into flames of fire or blades of grass.

Instructions – Large-leaf Philodendron

Because you are making mirror images, remember that 2 fabrics will make half of a leaf. Thus, to get 2 leaves, turn 2 fabrics right-side up and 2 fabrics wrong-side up.

Using the four 6" x 9" fabric rectangles, turn the 2nd and 4th fabrics wrong-side up (Fig. 5–10). The wrong side of prints with definite right and wrong sides is easier to see; however, if you are using only batiks, this will not matter because you can flip the fabric to either side prior to stitching.

RIGHT: **Fig. 5–10:** These 4 fabric rectangles with fabrics #2 and #4 are shown wrong-side up. Press fabrics together in pairs or altogether in preparation for rotary curvy cutting.

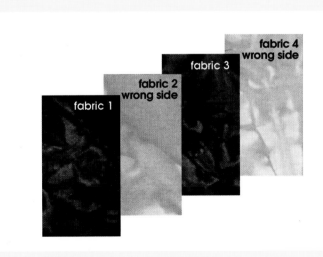

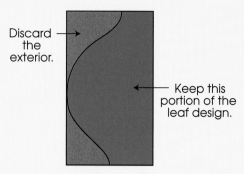

Discard the exterior.

Keep this portion of the leaf design.

Fig. 5–11: Stack 4 fabrics to execute an exterior rotary cut.

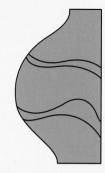

Fig. 5–12: Rotary cut 2 or 3 inset stems with gentle curves.

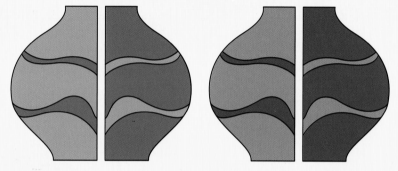

Fig. 5–13: Create a mock-up of 2 leaves with stems, each rectangle being half of a leaf.

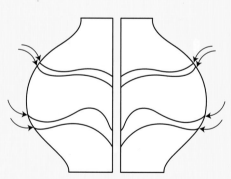

Fig. 5–14: When you are happy with your inset horizontal stem arrangement, sew them into the leaf backgrounds with a ⅛" seam allowance. Remember: begin sewing on the outside of the half leaf, not in the center.

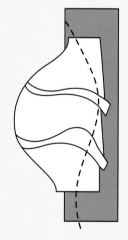

Fig. 5–15: This sketch shows the scrap (pink) for the center stem under the left half of the leaf. Dotted lines indicate where to make the first curvy cut.

Rotary cut the exterior curve of only half of a philodendron leaf, discarding the portion that is not part of the leaf shape (Figs. 5–11 and 5–12).

Repeat until all the side stems are inset into the half-leaf formations, pressing aggressively after each seam is sewn into place (Fig. 5–13).

Note that the center of the leaf is not in proportion yet; the top and bottom are larger than they should be when the leaf is complete. Such extra fabric allows for the center stem to be rotary cut *after* you've finished stitching the side stems (Fig. 5–14).

The last element to create is the center stem. After all the side stems are sewn into place, find a long slender scrap of fabric (approximately 2" to 3" wide x a little longer than the length of the center of the leaf). Place this scrap under and to the right of the left half of the leaf (Fig. 5–15). The slender scrap may be different from any fabrics already used for your leaf. Remember: this is imaginary!

Rotary cut a gentle curve through both the left half-leaf and the slender scrap. Taper the cut towards the tip of the leaf. Stitch with a ⅛" seam allowance and press aggressively.

Repeat for the right side, but try to slightly offset the side stems above or below the left side stems so that they do not match—just like a real leaf. It may be necessary to add to the length of the right half (Fig. 5–16).

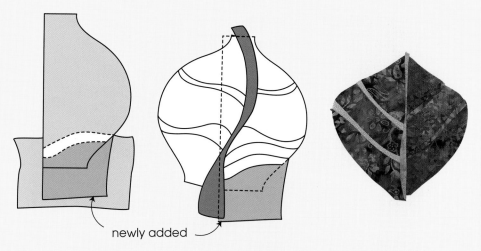

newly added

Fig. 5–16: Dotted lines show how to add fabric if needed. Make another cut within the insert. Stitch the new unit to the bottom of the leaf. Move the right side until the horizontal stems are offset. Discard the area shown by the dotted line. Sew together.

Large-leaf Philodendron Quilts Gallery

Large, outsized scale, humongous, big—honestly, really BIG—appeals to me! For example, our yard adapts well to vast and generous proportions whether that be in flowers, shrubs, and/or hardscapes. Large leaves such as those found on a *Paulownia* (aka Princess Tree or Empress Tree) are incredibly beautiful and lush. They were the inspiration for my quilt called, what else, ONE BIG HONKING LEAF WITH FRIENDS.

This piece has netting used as batting. A couple of sources for materials were used. Many of these fabrics were found in the dress department of a fabric store but others were found at my favorite shopping place—a Goodwill® store. Sometimes the most incredible glitz may be found in the long gown area where some dresses are yards and yards of fabric and not much money.

ABOVE: ONE BIG HONKING LEAF WITH FRIENDS, approximately 29" x 29", made by the author. A little glitz, some sleazy fabric, a scrunch of netting for batting, and I think somebody had way too much fun creating this oversized leaf!

LEFT: Not only did Margaret design a wonderful quilt, she sent me a fabutantastic postcard using a leaf. I loved it, and thereby the postcard was named! FABUTANTASTIC POST-CARD (I named it!), 8¾" x 5¾", sent to me by Margaret Hunt, Clarks Hill, South Carolina. What a great leftover from her quilt.

RIGHT: Janet Myers of Flandreau, South Dakota, designed a wonderful quilt, LEAVES 1, 39" x 56". Everything about it makes me smile with joy. The changing shapes are inspired and the hanging leaves give delicate balance as finished embellishments to her quilt.

LEFT: Jody Wigton of Columbus, Ohio, created big leaves and used the same curvy method for oak and maple leaf simulations in FUNKY FAUNA, 52" x 29". The leaves are appliquéd onto a fall-colored background.

RIGHT: As far as I know, the first big honking leaves made for this book were created by Margaret Hunt of Clarks Hill, South Carolina, in LEAVES, approximately 48" x 23".

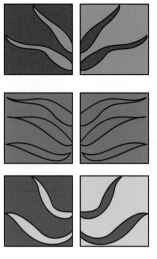

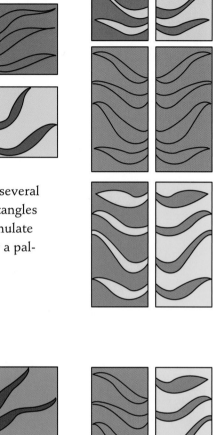

Fig. 5–17: Sew several squares or rectangles together to simulate palm leaves or a palmetto branch.

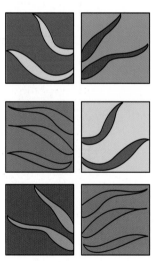

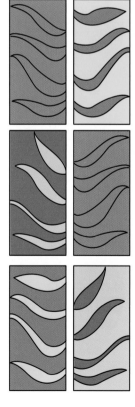

Fig. 5–18: Consider the square arrangement: light backgrounds are on the right, dark on the left. In the rectangular set, the light or dark backgrounds are mixed.

Instructions – Palm Leaves

I suggest that 6 fabrics be chosen in shades of either 3 darks with 3 mediums, or 3 mediums with 3 lights. This contrast simulates the light behind the slender palmetto. If you select 3 darks with 3 lights, the contrast could be too stark.

When curvy cutting, work with only 2 fabrics at a time—a lighter and a darker one— and turn one of the two face-down. Create 3 sets of curvies in different curvy designs. Figure 5–17 shows the 2 partners arranged across from each other. They are partners in design and in colorway—an excellent way to group the blocks.

What if you were to mix up the partnerships as in figure 5–18? The design movement would change. The paired design is more straight-laced, proper, and is "in place," whereas the mixed arrangement looks like the fronds are in wind movement. Both are good; neither is wrong. Keep in mind that, as always, it is your choice as to how your arrangement works best for you and makes your heart happy.

Lay out the background first and then insert a variety of leaves. If you need more variety, fussy-cut more leaves. Often a medley of different fabrics is the punch needed to make a piece sing. Why not create a frond with a combination of squares and rectangles?

Sew the blocks into 2 columns, leaving the right-hand side of one unit and the left-hand side of the other ragged. Apply the curly-curvies techniques on page 62 to create a curved center stem. Once the top is complete, trim the edges, square it up, add more blocks—do whatever speaks to you!

OPPOSITE: Saffron, detail, full quilt page 80

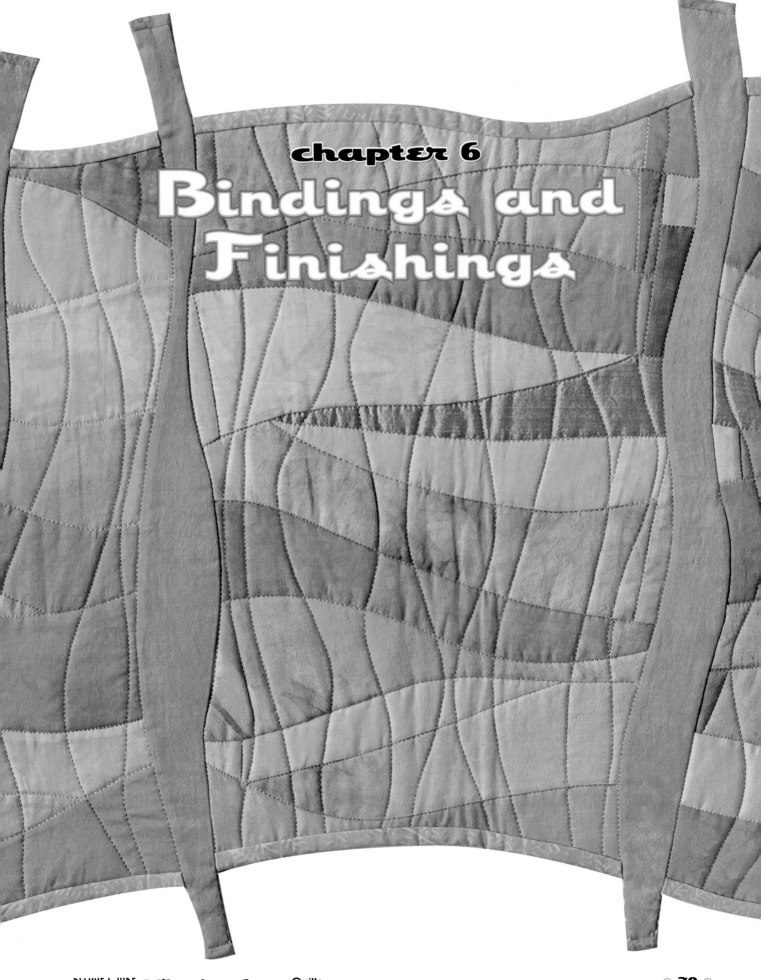

chapter 6
Bindings and Finishings

a question so often asked of me is, "How do you bind all those pointy things that stand up out of your quilts?" Well, I figure it out as I go. Really, it's like a jigsaw puzzle and I like to work those.

Let's give those pointy things a name to make reading and writing easier. How about *stick-outs?* They are not always stick-ups, nor are they always stick-downs, but certainly they are always stick-outs, whether from the top, bottom, or sides.

As I began to finish SAFFRON with its orange stick-outs, it occurred to me that now would be a perfect time to document and photograph how these pointy things are bound. So, here we go—and know that I was actually binding this quilt as I wrote these instructions.

You must determine which is best for your quilt—a bias- or straight-cut binding. Ordinarily, if the quilt's edges are going to be curvy, I use a bias-cut binding. If the edges are straight, I go for a straight-cut binding. Now, don't hold me to that; there are times when I've done the absolute opposite for one or both of those situations since nothing is written in granite. Always pushing the perpetual envelope has offered me many new ways of doing basic quilting techniques.

Both types of bindings are excellent, but I suggest that in most cases, a double layer of fabric is a better choice for your binding than single.

For a double binding to finish at ¼", which is my preference, cut strips 2½", fold them in half, and trim them to 1". By the time you sew the binding

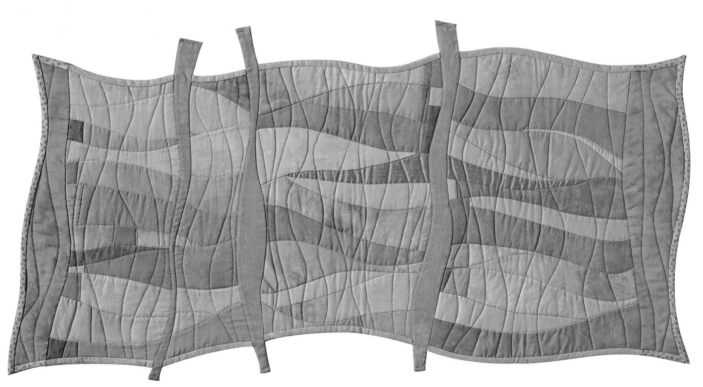

ABOVE: SAFFRON, 36" x 18", made by the author, has those strange pointy things at the top and bottom. The same binding process applies if you opt to point them out of your quilt left or right.

a ¼" seam, the apparent mathematical discrepancy will have disappeared into the same place where missing socks go and your quilt will be lovely. Bindings ¼" wide are narrow enough to allow a pleasing curve and wide enough to make a statement for the quilt.

If the quilt is bulky, loosely zigzag around its perimeter. Take care to stitch without stretching the edges.

With an extra ¼" at the start and the end of the binding, begin stitching a ¼" seam at the first arrow where the stick-out starts (Fig. 6–1). End at the next arrow. Begin and end with a few backstitches to hold the binding in place.

Press the binding away from the quilt. Pressing makes for a cleaner turn around the quilt face. Repeat this process until the entire quilt has bindings stitched between all the stick-outs (Fig. 6–2 through Fig. 6–10).

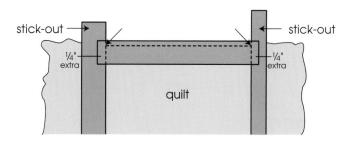

Fig. 6–1: The extra ¼" of fabric on both ends is to turn under after the binding is stitched. Arrows point to where stitching begins and ends.

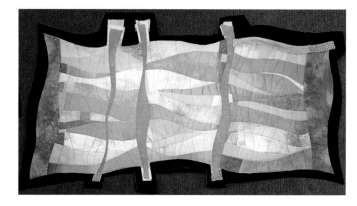

Fig. 6–2: This shows the quilt with only 1 binding (right, top) stitched into place.

Fig. 6–3: This detail shows the left side without bindings. It has been rotary cut to the curvy shape that I want. Note that the stick-outs have batting larger than the yellow upright stick-outs. The batting will serve as a folding/cutting guide later (see text page 83).

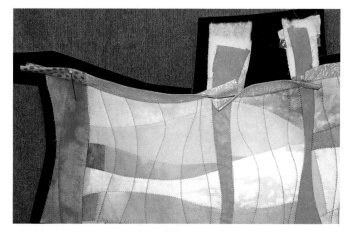

Fig. 6–4: Bindings are sewn onto the quilt's front. Address the stick-outs later.

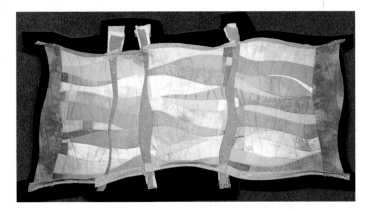

Fig. 6–5: All of the horizontal bindings have been sewn onto the top and bottom of the quilt.

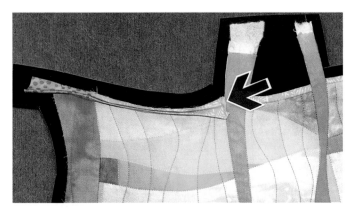

Fig. 6–6: The 2 right-handed horizontal bindings are hemstitched (complete). The arrow shows the last binding (left) folded back, ready to hemstitch onto the back of the quilt.

Fig. 6–7: The back of the quilt is shown with 2 bindings complete and one sewn only to the front. This last binding is ready to bring to the back of the quilt and hemstitch.

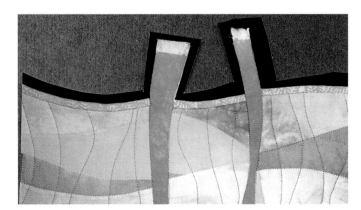

Fig. 6–8: The top of quilt has the bindings hemstitched and in place, bound nicely. The stick-outs have not been bound yet.

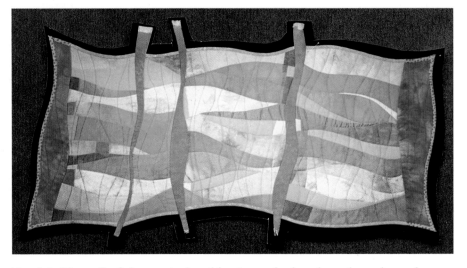

Fig. 6–9: Now all of the vertical and horizontal edges have been bound.

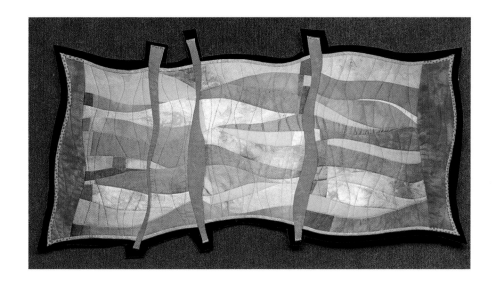

To bind the stick-outs, take it slowly, and address only one stick-out at a time. This will mentally free you up from thinking of the larger task, especially if you have a large quilt with many stick-outs. It's very rewarding when you accomplish each little step, especially when the completed product looks so pleasing and professional.

Fold the stick-out on the desired stitching line toward the back of the quilt (Fig. 6–11). This creates a line that guides the cutting of the batting (Fig. 6–12).

Carefully cut the 2 sides of the batting to fit underneath the front layer of the stick-out. Take care to cut only the batting and not the front or back fabrics.

Go to the back of the quilt, trim a bit, and fold the backing fabric over the right and left sides of the cut batting.

By hand and with a blindstitch, attach the front fabric to the back, covering the backing fabric.

Turn under the stick-out's binding when it intersects (touches) the quilt's binding. Here you may need to do a little connecting stitch to hold these two together and to cover any raw threads.

The end of each stick-out is bound last. By leaving these until last, you have the creative option of changing the stick-out lengths. This is important. Only when all other edges are finished will you know what the best length should be because the visual proportions may change. These ends are easy to bind in your normal way.

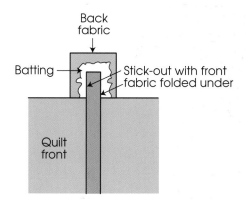

Fig. 6–11: Front layer on fold

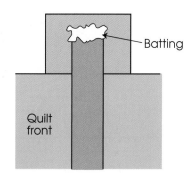

Fig. 6–12: Cut batting using the front layer's fold as a guide.

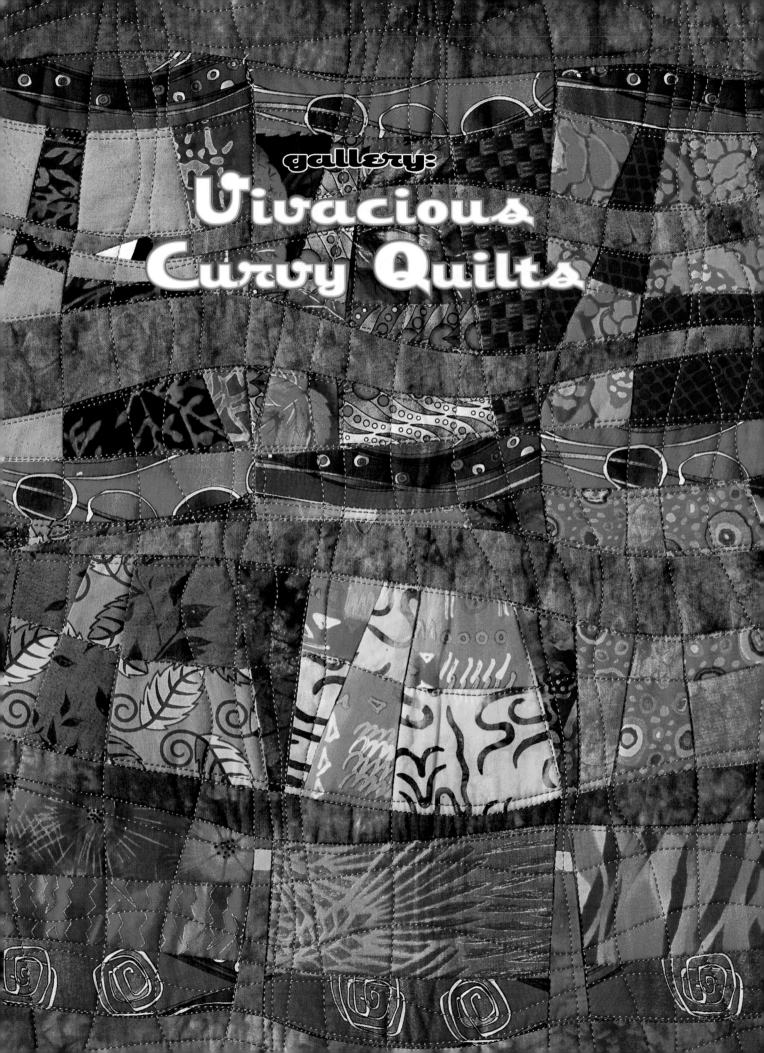

gallery:
Vivacious
Curvy Quilts

LEFT: SAPPHIRE, 26" x 28", is my experiment with two things: first, to only sew vertical curves to the quilt; and second, to use only one color, albeit as many shades of that color as possible. Instead of stacking several fabrics, each new fabric was curvy cut individually and then added in place. I continued doing this until the quilt said, "STOP! No More. That's enough." Believe me, it pays to listen when a quilt speaks that loudly. However, SAPPHIRE asks to be displayed horizontally. OK, quilt.

RIGHT: CURVED HAPPENSTANCE, 22" x 19", made by the author, is a chance discovery quilt. The background was begun as an example of a quilt-block game (Puzzler) from *Quilters Playtime,* but ended up being whacked with curvies. Look at the horizontal olive fabrics. They cross over curvy verticals. As intended, the horizontals become the dominant design element with the Puzzler being a recessive background.

OPPOSITE: CURVED HAPPENSTANCE, detail

I was writing the last chapter of *Vivacious Curvy Quilts* when a note arrived from Janet Myers, one of the book's quiltmakers. She included an image of yet another one of her quilts and I went crazy for it. LEAVES 2 is approximately 58" x 63". Each block is well-thought out, and the overall composite hangs together beautifully. Note the wild-colored zippers that may be unzipped to look through!

CURVACEOUS SHAPES: "OUT-OF-CONTROL," approximately 54" x 54",
was made by the author and is owned by Barbara Daggett of Lincolnville,
Maine, and Eustis, Florida. On the design wall this quilt had all these
incredibly strange, hanging, dangling, and very weird things pinned onto a
many-layered background. My husband walked into the room and quietly
(almost to himself) said, "Okay, this time you are totally out-of-control!"
Didn't I laugh and tell him he had just named the quilt? It was a moment.

LEFT: STARRY, STARRY NIGHTS is my curvy interpretation of a straight-pieced, traditional Star block used by the Northern Star Quilters of Somers, New York, as their chapter logo. It seemed natural to turn it into a curved variation. The circular centers are 3-D stuffed circles on their way to making this quilt go supernova at any minute.

BELOW: RAINDROP MELODY: LINDA'S QUILT, 30" x 18", was made by the author and is owned by Linda Doran of Nashville, Tennessee. This little quilt includes not only curvy techniques but also a game, Checker-Border—the black-and-white bordering from *Quilters Playtime*. It is curvy-pieced and machine appliquéd.

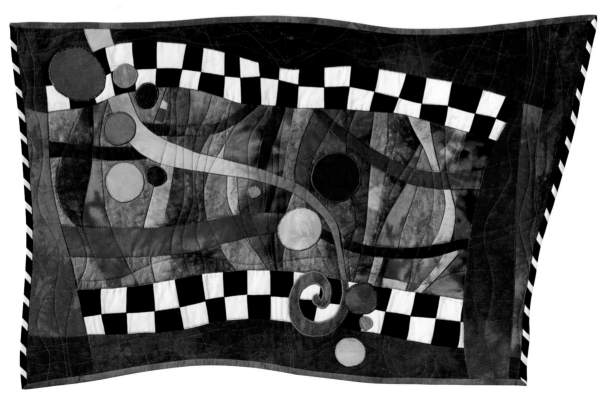

RIGHT: LOOSE CURVES, approximately 64" x 64", is another color exploration. This time, I created several little quilts in basically one color, but this time the little quilts said, "Don't STOP!—keep going." It became really interesting after the nine little quilts were completed. What, exactly, would be a worthy housing? The idea that came to mind—open-worked lattice created with only vertical components—couldn't be done. The quilt actually imploded upon itself.

LEFT: After returning to the University of Hard Rocks for an engineering degree in fabric and quilt construction *(jest kiddin')*, I think the back of LOOSE CURVES is nearly as much fun as the front. It, too, has an interlacing lattice effect. See how the nine little quilts show up as color-blocks sitting on a lattice-like framework.

LEFT: I designed and stitched WHICH WAY IS UP?, 80" x 86", and donated it to our local quilt guild for a fund-raiser. Joan Herrick, another member, donated her intricate, well-executed, and well-designed machine quilting. The almost-open framework of 16 interwoven units are made of hand-dyes (or look like they are), and are placed on a curvy-pieced background of mustard yellow—a new neutral, if you ask me. The quilt was raffled and the new owner is Charlotte R. Ouellette of Belfast, Maine.
PHOTO: PHIL CARTHAGE

RIGHT: SEURAT'S DOTS AND ZYDECO, 65" x 81", is an imaginary interpretation of Seurat's pointillist technique should he meet up with a New Orleans jazz band playing the rhythmic sounds of Zydeco. Working with only dotted fabrics, I used the side-to-opposite-side curvy cut (see page 18) but made a secondary cut in each block. By putting the reds and yellows into the center (a rectangular shape) and then surrounding the edges with navy, hunter green, and sage green, the colors began to show themselves. It is in the collection of the International Quilt Festival, Houston, Texas; used by permission of Karey Bresenhan.
PHOTO: TERRY HIRE

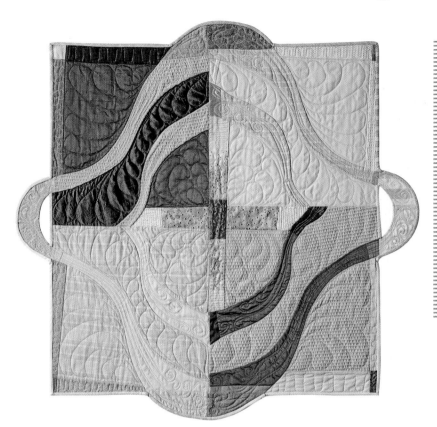

LEFT: The title for A LIGHT UNTO MY PATH, 38" x 39½", is from Psalm 119: 105: "Your word is a lamp unto my feet and a light unto my path." This book has taken far more years than I care to enumerate due to many physical upsets to my body. This quilt, with a pathway surrounding a central cross in every conceivable shade of white to signify restoration and light, is symbolic of an eternity without any hurts or pains, with every tear wiped away, where God will reign. On my desk is taped another verse: "God will make this happen, for He who calls you is faithful." 1 Thess. 5:24. I believe it.

The warm months in Maine find me occupied with what I lovingly call "my summer piecing"— working with rocks. When the air is warm and sun is shining, being inside is like being locked in prison. My husband and I garden together, working out the designs in curved flower beds (more curvy piecing) as well as curved pathways throughout the garden, and I lay rocks. You see, rocks are nothing but larger 3-dimensional fabrics; placing them is the same as piecing fabrics, so why not lay rocks? This particular "quilt," *Tribute to Andy,* 8' x 6', is named for Andy Goldsworthy, known for his cairns in Dumfries, Scotland, and was built by the author. PHOTOS: TERRY HIRE

Acknowledgments

*a*t the beginning of creating a book, the journey is never a one-person endeavor. To birth any book, the process takes several sequential steps.

First, secure fabric. To begin, I thank Donna Wilder. Her encouragement over the last several years has offered not only colorfully designed fabrics but gentle words to continue walking when walking almost seemed impossible. I also enjoy touching and holding and purchasing from such dyers as Melody Johnson, Laura Wasilowski, Jo Coons, Ricky Tims, and many other unnamed dye artists all over the country.

A quilt is more than a surface of pieced-together fabrics. Wonder-Under® fusible web by Pellon has been the product for which I always reach when more stabilizing is needed. A quilt's middle layer must be addressed, too. I congratulate Fairfield Processing Corporation on their company's continuous desire to create the softest, most plush, and best battings on the market and thank them for the sharing of those batts.

Tools, of course are important. Olfa – North America, Division of World Kitchen, LLC, must be thanked for sending their latest and greatest product goodies. My thanks to Carl R. Cottrell II, national accounts manager, for his support of quiltmaking by furnishing many excellent tools over the last several years.

How about a sewing machine? I have been a 20+ year BERNINA user. When Janome America,

OPPOSITE: CROP CIRCLES, detail, full quilt shown on page 57

Inc., offered one of theirs, I could only sit back and wait to see if one worked for me. Marie Stevens of Janome convinced me to try it. To Alison Newman, Marketing Coordinator, I offer thanks because the Janome works very well. So, with a hug, I retired dear Lady Bernie, who watches over my work today from her shelf, and I still love her for many years of diligent, hard work.

To all the quiltmakers who have joined me along the curvy trail, I offer sincere thanks; your enduring patience awaiting this book's birthing and publication is much appreciated. Quilts created by you have added designs, dimensions, and color palettes to this book that I may never have considered.

That brings up the ability of AQS Publishing to tolerate my delays. Thank you, Meredith Schroeder. You have been more than understanding; you have gone beyond any word to describe *undemanding* in the process to bring forth this book. And a special thanks to Andi Reynolds, my editor, whose soft voice uplifts. Without her gentle pushing, the copy would still be in rough-draft form, dying of old age, and the quilts would have graying strings hanging down. Thank you, Andi.

The last thing I mention was actually the first step in the process—the idea for this book. Fellow quiltmaker Nancy R. Board showed me a simple curved demonstration triggering the first hint of a doable technique. Developing the method further, I had a faint light-bulb glimmer of this curvy book. It goes without saying that I offer my genuine thanks to you, Nancy, wherever you are.

Dianne

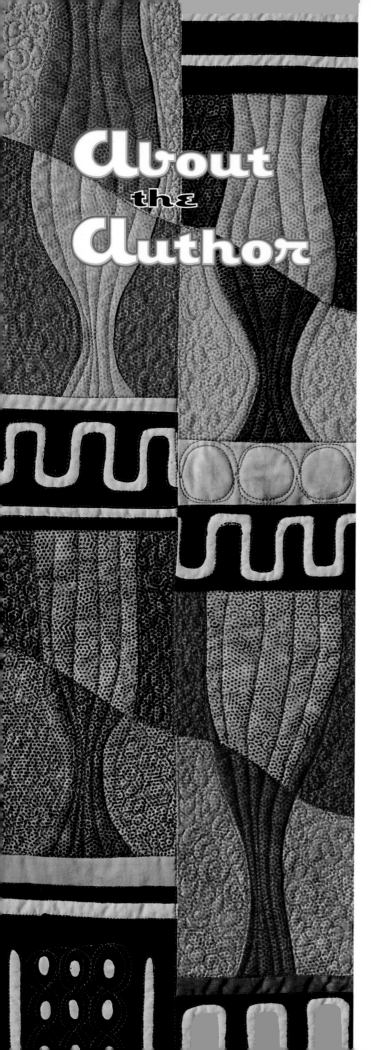

About the Author

PHOTO: TERRY HIRE

When asked for a bio for this book, Dianne said, "Oh, just tell 'em that I have the coloring sense of a first grader."

Combine such color freedom with her artistic design sense and you will see creations that are deceptively simple but visually exciting. She makes quilts that sometimes reflect the influence of her prior profession as a couture dress buyer. Blend the works of Halston plus Oscar de la Renta, then Koos Van Den Akker plus Geoffrey Beene, and then Ralph Lauren plus Anne Klein and you're on to Dianne's style. She incorporates simplicity of design with her childlike color sense plus beautifully applied embellishments to create interesting, intuitively designed quilts.

An international exhibitor, award-winning quilter, lecturer, instructor, and author, Dianne's quirky sense of humor is fun to be around. She writes as she speaks, using a language unpredictably interesting yet easily understood. Her previous AQS books are *Oxymorons: Absurdly Logical Quilts!* (2001) and *Quilters Playtime: Games with Fabrics* (2004).

Dianne lives with her husband, Terry, in Northport, Maine, where they are supervised by Sir Hilary, who graces the dedication page. A cat's work never ends.

LEFT: RESTORED GOBLETS, detail, full quilt page 29

Index: quiltmakers and quilts

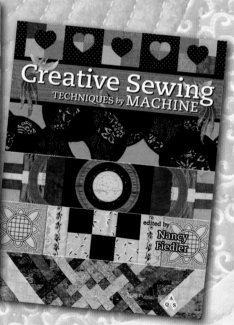

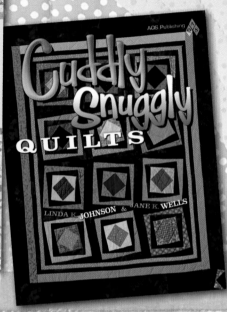